The Ultimate Runner's Journal

YOUR DAILY TRAINING PARTNER AND LOG

by Rich Hanna

Capital Road Race Publications (CRRP)
Sacramento, California

THE ULTIMATE RUNNER'S JOURNAL © copyright 2003 by Rich Hanna, Second Edition

10 9 8 7 6 5 4 3 2 1

Cover photograph © David Madison Sports Images, Incorporated.

Before beginning any new training program, or before following the advice of the articles contained in this book, consult your physician to ensure you can do so safely. These articles are in no way intended to substitute for medical advice.

ISBN 0-9655187-9-5

Distributed to the book trade by Independent Publishers Group (800.888.4741).

Individuals may order directly from the publisher, Capital Road Race Publications (916.492.8966), but please check your local bookstore first.

Personal Information

Name ....

Address ....

....

....

Phone # ....

Allergies ....

Emergency contact information ....

....

....

Goals for the year ....

....

....

....

....

....

....

....

....

New to the sport of marathoning,
Herbert was a little confused when told
to always keep a training log.

Contents

Introduction

Hundreds of books are available on the sport of running. Perhaps none is more valuable for your running success than the one you will author with the help of the book you are holding right now — *The Ultimate Runner's Journal*. *The Ultimate Runner's Journal* is the most comprehensive running log on the market today. It contains all of the objective categories that you need to monitor and chart your training and racing including: route, mileage, time, heart rate, cross training, and workout. The unique daily goal section keeps you focused and encourages you to plan for reaching your fitness goals. The notes section gives you double the writing space of conventional logbooks so even the most analytical among us can wax on about a terrific tempo run and/or complain about an achy Achilles.

The heart of any running log, of course, is the log sheet. *The Ultimate Runner's Journal* contains a good one. But further separating *The Journal* from the competition are the other added extras that accompany each page. You'll find cutting-edge advice from some of the top minds in the sport, like Jack Daniels, Sally Edwards and Mary Coordt. Their wisdom and advice gives you ideas that you can put to immediate use. In addition, you will likely get a chuckle from several running cartoons conceptualized by clever cartoonist Doug Hanna and brought to life by ace-animator Jeff Edwards. You'll find more humor, and considerable running wisdom, in Joe Kelly's "53 Runner's Commandments" and Tim Martin's "Runner's Log: A Runner's Retreat." To help you track whether you are meeting your running goals, the weekly Goal Map will give you an at-a-glance comparison of each day's scheduled run to compare with your actual workouts. Finally, each week leads off with a thought-provoking, motivational, or funny quote intended to motivate you further toward your goals. Hopefully you can take away a bit of wisdom, or at least get a laugh, from some of them.

So, here it is. A state-of-the art running journal just waiting for you to personalize it with your training and racing data, thoughts, and experiences. See you out there!

PART I

The Articles

Some running injuries are not caused from over-training.

Daniels On Training*

by Jack Daniels, Ph.D.

When I was struggling to become a better runner, there was nowhere to turn for sound advice. I even searched the grocery checkout lines, but couldn't find anything that promised to improve my mile time by 20 seconds in 20 days. I attended coaching convention after convention, but seldom did I hear about sound principles of training: how to set up a season program, how much or how fast to train, and how programs differ. Throughout my career as an Olympic athlete, exercise scientist, and running coach, I've been looking for answers to these questions, as are most runners and coaches today.

In the following pages I distill the results of my lifelong search. For a fuller discussion of these and other training principles, please turn to my book, *Daniels' Running Formula* (Human Kinetics, 1998).

The Goals of Training

When taking the step from "just running" to training, a runner is trying to accomplish the following:

- Improve the body's ability to transport blood and oxygen
- Increase the ability of the running muscles to utilize their available oxygen effectively (to convert carbohydrate and fat fuel into useful energy)
- Increase the runner's maximum oxygen consumption (VO2Max), which is the sum of the first two above
- Shift lactate threshold to correspond to a faster running speed
- Improve speed
- Lower the energy demand of running (improve economy)

Specific types of training should be used to optimize each of these components of performance. It is critical that before you take your first step, you know the exact purpose of that particular run. My suggested types of training follow.

Types of Training

Easy and Long Runs. When you do easy (E) runs to recover from strenuous periods of training or to carry out a second workout on a particular day, and when you do your long (L) runs, you should run at a pace that corresponds to 65% to 75% of your maximum heart rate (MaxHR). Long runs, up to 2-1/2 hours, improve cell adaptation and lead to glycogen depletion and fluid loss (important considerations for distance runners), but should not be demanding in terms of the intensity (pace).

The benefits of E-pace running are more a function of time spent exercising than intensity of running, so do not exceed 75% of your MaxHR or you will be working harder than necessary to reap the intended benefits to the heart muscle and cells.

Marathon-Pace Runs. The next faster intensity of training is marathon race pace (MP) and is limited to marathon training. Your MP is the pace at which you plan to race your next marathon, and is about 20 to 30 seconds per mile slower than threshold (T) pace.

Threshold-Pace Runs. Threshold pace (T) is about 90% of MaxHR. Subjectively, T pace is "comfortably-hard" running. It is important to stay as close as possible to the prescribed speed; neither slower nor faster velocities do as good a job as does the proper speed. T-pace training improves your lactate threshold.

Interval-Pace Runs. The next important training velocity, interval pace (I), is the one that stresses and improves VO2Max. The intensity should be equal to about 98% to 100% of MaxHR. No single interval should exceed 5 minutes. Interval training is demanding, but by no means is it all-out running. In the case of I pace, the harm of going too fast is that no better results are obtained and the excessive pace will probably leave you overstressed for the next quality training session (or injured).

Repetition Pace. Repetition (R) velocity is faster than I pace, but unlike I and T running, is not based on VO2Max. Rather, R pace is to a great extent based on the race for which you are training; it is more designed for good mechanics at a pretty fast pace. Keep in mind that the purpose of R-pace training is to improve economy and speed, not to benefit VO2Max or lactate threshold.

Avoiding Quality-Junk Training. As you can see from Figure 1, there is a shaded area between I and T, and T and E/L. These are the "no-man's land" of training. With the exception of MP runs (which do fall in "no-man's land" between E/L and T), running at an intensity that falls in the shaded areas is either too slow or too hard to reap the benefits you want. You are not achieving the purpose of training by going faster or slower than the chosen intensity. What you are doing might be termed "quality-junk" training.

Determining Your Fitness

Now that you understand my suggested types of training, you need to determine your level of fitness so you can train at the appropriate pace for each training type. By using standard

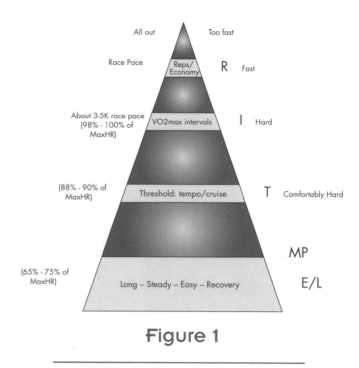

Figure 1

values for running economy and by having a timed performance over at least one running distance, a fitness (VDOT) value can be assigned to you for training and race-prediction purposes. Table 1 on page 12 provides this information. To use this VDOT table, you merely look up a time associated with a distance you have recently raced (or run hard) and read across to the column headed by "VDOT". VDOT is an adjusted VO2Max which tells you how you might race for other distances (in a row associated

Aerobic Profile

VO2Submax. Let's say we have a runner who has reached a "steady state" of exercise by running for about six minutes at a submaximal speed (8:00 per mile pace, for example) and a bag of expired air is collected from this runner during the final minute or two of this six-minute run. The analysis of the expired air will tell us what the aerobic (oxygen) demand of running at 8:00 pace is for this runner. Heart rate, also taken during the final minute or two of the run, and a small finger-stick blood sample (drawn immediately upon completion of the run) will provide information on the heart rate and blood-lactate accumulation associated with this velocity of running for this individual.

If the runner completes three or four submax tests (at increasingly faster speeds, up to about 10K race pace or a little faster), and then performs a "max" test, the response picture becomes adequate for determining current training and even competitive intensities of running.

Velocity at VO2Max. By adding the highest VO2 measured during the max test (this is VO2Max) and the MaxHR and BlaMax (blood lactate accumulation), we get the runner's aerobic profile. Now we can determine the velocity (or pace) at which VO2Max would first be realized. This velocity is simply called vVO2Max (velocity at VO2Max) and is used to calculate a VDOT value, which in turn determines training paces and race potential.

with the same VDOT), and also tells you how fast to perform different types of training.

Table 2 on pages 13 and 14 provides the training intensity information. Also notice that marathon pace (MP) is shown here. When using a current VDOT to determine training intensities, you plug the identified VDOT (from Table 1) into Table 2 and read across that row to identify paces for E/L runs, T runs, I workouts, and R training.

Now that you know your training paces, you need to set up your training program.

Creating Your Training Program

My preferred approach to an ideal 24-week season of training is 4 6-week phases with a few races spread throughout the final three phases of training. The first is a foundation/injury-prevention (FI) phase, consisting mostly of E and L runs and some strides thrown in.

For most runners, the second phase, which I call early quality (EQ), is primarily designed to work on mechanics, economy and some speed—a Repetition (R) phase. Some examples of R workouts are hill training, fartleks, and two-minute or less repetitions at R pace.

Phase three (Transition Quality—TQ) is the toughest segment and concentrates on long intervals. Note that individual runs making up an interval session should never last longer than 5 minutes each.

The final (Final Quality—FQ) phase involves a fair amount of threshold running, along with little, if any, R or I work. Examples of threshold running are tempo runs (a steady 20-minute run at T pace) and cruise intervals (repeated runs at T pace of anywhere from 3 to 10 minutes, broken up by short recovery periods).

Organizing the types of training to emphasize in each phase is largely dependent upon the event(s) being trained for, with shorter races demanding more repetitions later in the season

Table 1

VDOT VALUES

VDOT	Mile	5K	10K	15K	13.1M	26.2M		VDOT	Mile	5K	10K	15K	13.1M	26.2M
30	9:11	30:40	1:03:46	1:38:14	2:21:04	4:49:17		58	5:06	17:33	36:24	55:55	1:20:30	2:48:14
31	8:55	29:51	1:02:03	1:35:36	2:17:21	4:41:57		59	5:02	17:17	35:52	55:06	1:19:18	2:45:47
32	8:41	29:05	1:00:26	1:33:07	2:13:49	4:34:59		60	4:57	17:03	35:22	54:18	1:18:09	2:43:25
33	8:27	28:21	58:54	1:30:45	2:10:27	4:28:22		61	4:53	16:48	34:52	53:32	1:17:02	2:41:08
34	8:14	27:39	57:26	1:28:30	2:07:16	4:22:03		62	4:49	16:34	34:23	52:47	1:15:57	2:38:54
35	8:01	27:00	56:03	1:26:22	2:04:13	4:16:03		63	4:45	16:20	33:55	52:03	1:14:54	2:36:44
36	7:49	26:22	54:44	1:24:20	2:01:19	4:10:19		64	4:41	16:07	33:28	51:21	1:13:53	2:34:38
37	7:38	25:46	53:29	1:22:24	1:58:34	4:04:50		65	4:37	15:54	33:01	50:40	1:12:53	2:32:35
38	7:27	25:12	52:17	1:20:33	1:55:55	3:59:35		66	4:33	15:42	32:35	50:00	1:11:56	2:30:36
39	7:17	24:39	51:09	1:18:47	1:53:24	3:54:34		67	4:30	15:29	32:11	49:22	1:11:00	2:28:40
40	7:07	24:08	50:03	1:17:06	1:50:59	3:49:45		68	4:26	15:18	31:46	48:44	1:10:05	2:26:47
41	6:58	23:38	49:01	1:15:29	1:48:40	3:45:09		69	4:23	15:06	31:23	48:08	1:09:12	2:24:57
42	6:49	23:09	48:01	1:13:56	1:46:27	3:40:43		70	4:19	14:55	31:00	47:32	1:08:21	2:23:10
43	6:41	22:41	47:04	1:12:27	1:44:20	3:36:28		71	4:16	14:44	30:38	46:58	1:07:31	2:21:26
44	6:32	22:15	46:09	1:11:02	1:42:17	3:32:23		72	4:13	14:33	30:16	46:24	1:06:42	2:19:44
45	6:25	21:50	45:16	1:09:40	1:40:20	3:28:26		73	4:10	14:23	29:55	45:51	1:05:54	2:18:05
46	6:17	21:25	44:25	1:08:22	1:38:27	3:24:39		74	4:06	14:13	29:34	45:19	1:05:08	2:16:29
47	6:10	21:02	43:36	1:07:06	1:36:38	3:21:00		75	4:04	14:03	29:14	44:48	1:04:23	2:14:55
48	6:03	20:39	42:50	1:05:53	1:34:53	3:17:29		76	4:02	13:54	28:55	44:18	1:03:39	2:13:23
49	5:56	20:18	42:04	1:04:44	1:33:12	3:14:06		77	3:58	13:44	28:36	43:49	1:02:56	2:11:54
50	5:50	19:57	41:21	1:03:36	1:31:35	3:10:49		78	3:56.2	13:35	28:17	43:20	1:02:15	2:10:27
51	5:44	19:36	40:39	1:02:31	1:30:02	3:07:39		79	3:53.7	13:26	27:59	42:52	1:01:34	2:09:02
52	5:38	19:17	39:59	1:01:29	1:28:31	3:04:36		80	3:51.2	13:17.8	27:41	42:25	1:00:54	2:07:38
53	5:32	18:58	39:20	1:00:28	1:27:04	3:01:39		81	3:48.7	13:09.3	27:24	41:58	1:00:15	2:06:17
54	5:27	18:40	38:42	59:30	1:25:40	2:58:47		82	3:46.4	13:01.1	27:07	41:32	59:38	2:04:57
55	5:21	18:22	38:06	58:33	1:24:18	2:56:01		83	3:44.1	12:53	26:51	41:06	59:01	2:03:40
56	5:16	18:05	37:31	57:39	1:23:00	2:53:20		84	3:41.8	12:45.2	26:34	40:42	58:25	2:02:24
57	5:11	17:49	36:57	56:46	1:21:43	2:50:45		85	3:39.6	12:37.4	26:19	40:17	57:50	2:01:10

Table 2

VDOT	E/L Pace mile	MP mile	T Pace 400	T Pace 1000	T Pace mile	I Pace 400	I Pace 1000	I Pace 1200	I Pace mile	R Pace 200	R Pace 400	R Pace 800
30	12:16	11:02	2:33	6:24	10:18	2:22	–	–	–	67	2:16	–
32	11:41	10:29	2:26	6:05	9:47	2:14	–	–	–	63	2:08	–
34	11:09	10:00	2:19	5:48	9:20	2:08	–	–	–	60	2:02	–
36	10:40	9:33	2:13	5:33	8:55	2:02	5:07	–	–	57	1:55	–
38	10:14	9:08	2:07	5:19	8:33	1:56	4:54	–	–	54	1:50	–
40	9:50	8:46	2:02	5:06	8:12	1:52	4:42	–	–	52	1:46	–
42	9:28	8:25	1:57	4:54	7:52	1:48	4:31	–	–	50	1:42	–
44	9:07	8:06	1:53	4:43	7:33	1:44	4:21	–	–	48	98	–
45	8:58	7:57	1:51	4:38	7:25	1:42	4:16	–	–	47	96	–
46	8:48	7:48	1:49	4:33	7:17	1:40	4:12	5:00	–	46	94	–
47	8:39	7:40	1:47	4:29	7:10	98	4:07	4:54	–	45	92	–
48	8:31	7:32	1:45	4:24	7:02	96	4:03	4:49	–	44	90	–
49	8:22	7:24	1:43	4:20	6:55	95	3:59	4:45	–	44	89	–
50	8:14	7:17	1:42	4:15	6:51	93	3:55	4:41	–	43	87	–
51	8:07	7:09	1:40	4:11	6:44	92	3:51	4:36	–	42	86	–
52	7:59	7:02	98	4:07	6:38	91	3:48	4:33	–	42	85	–
53	7:52	6:56	97	4:04	6:32	90	3:44	4:29	–	41	84	–
54	7:45	6:49	95	4:00	6:26	88	3:41	4:25	–	40	82	–
55	7:38	6:43	94	3:56	6:20	87	3:37	4:21	–	40	81	–
56	7:31	6:37	93	3:53	6:15	86	3:34	4:18	–	39	80	–
57	7:25	6:31	91	3:50	6:09	85	3:31	4:15	–	39	79	–
58	7:19	6:25	90	3:45	6:04	83	3:28	4:10	–	38	77	–
59	7:13	6:19	89	3:43	5:59	82	3:25	4:07	–	37	76	–
60	7:07	6:14	88	3:40	5:54	81	3:23	4:03	–	37	75	2:30
61	7:01	6:09	86	3:37	5:50	80	3:20	4:00	–	36	74	2:28
62	6:56	6:04	85	3:34	5:45	79	3:17	3:57	–	36	73	2:26
63	6:50	5:59	84	3:32	5:41	78	3:15	3:54	–	35	72	2:24
64	6:45	5:54	83	3:29	5:36	77	3:12	3:51	–	35	71	2:22

Table 2 (con't)

TRAINING INTENSITIES

VDOT	E/L Pace mile	MP mile	T Pace 400	T Pace 1000	T Pace mile	I Pace 400	I Pace 1000	I Pace 1200	I Pace mile	R Pace 200	R Pace 400	R Pace 800
65	6:40	5:49	82	3:26	5:32	76	3:10	3:48	–	34	70	2:20
66	6:35	5:45	81	3:24	5:28	75	3:08	3:45	5:00	34	69	2:18
67	6:30	5:40	80	3:21	5:24	74	3:05	3:42	4:57	33	68	2:16
68	6:26	5:36	79	3:19	5:20	73	3:03	3:39	4:53	33	67	2:14
69	6:21	5:32	78	3:16	5:16	72	3:01	3:36	4:50	32	66	2:12
70	6:17	5:28	77	3:14	5:13	71	2:59	3:34	4:46	32	65	2:10
71	6:12	5:24	76	3:12	5:09	70	2:57	3:31	4:43	31	64	2:08
72	6:08	5:20	76	3:10	5:05	69	2:55	3:29	4:40	31	63	2:06
73	6:04	5:16	75	3:08	5:02	69	2:53	3:27	4:37	31	62	2:05
74	6:00	5:12	74	3:06	4:59	68	2:51	3:25	4:34	30	62	2:04
75	5:56	5:09	74	3:04	4:56	67	2:49	3:22	4:31	30	61	2:03
76	5:52	5:05	73	3:02	4:52	66	2:48	3:20	4:28	29	60	2:02
77	5:48	5:01	72	3:00	4:49	65	2:46	3:18	4:25	29	59	2:00
78	5:45	4:58	71	2:58	4:46	65	2:44	3:16	4:23	29	59	1:59
79	5:41	4:55	70	2:56	4:43	64	2:42	3:14	4:20	28	58	1:58
80	5:38	4:52	70	2:54	4:41	64	2:41	3:12	4:17	28	58	1:56
81	5:34	4:49	69	2:53	4:38	63	2:39	3:10	4:15	28	57	1:55
82	5:31	4:46	68	2:51	4:35	62	2:38	3:08	4:12	27	56	1:54
83	5:28	4:43	68	2:49	4:32	62	2:36	3:07	4:10	27	56	1:53
84	5:25	4:40	67	2:48	4:30	61	2:35	3:05	4:08	27	55	1:52
85	5:21	4:37	66	2:46	4:27	61	2:33	3:03	4:05	27	55	1:51

Stride Rate, a Step in the Right Direction

One of the first things I teach new runners is some basics about running cadence, or stride rate. I learned long ago that elite distance runners all tend to turnover at about the same rate—almost always 180 or more steps per minute. This means they are taking 90 or more steps with each foot each minute, a rate that doesn't vary too much even when not running very fast. The primary change that is made as a runner goes faster is in stride length; the faster they go the longer the stride becomes, with little change in leg turnover.

When I have my new running classes count their own stride rates I find that very few, if any, take as many as 180 steps per minute. In fact, some turnover as slowly as 160 times per minute. The main problem associated with a slower turnover is that you spend a longer time in the air, and the more time you are in the air, the higher you displace your body mass and the harder you hit the ground upon landing. And, when you figure that many running injuries are the result of excessive landing shock, it is not surprising that experienced runners all tend to turnover faster than do individuals who are new to the sport.

If you count your own stride rate and it is considerably slower than what I am suggesting, try to work on a shorter, lighter stride. Imagine you are running over a field of raw eggs and you don't want to break any of them—run over the ground, not into it. If you feel you need practice improving your stride rate, concentrate on it during easy runs. Rate usually goes up for slower turnover people when they race shorter distances, so often the need to think about it is not there during faster quality training. But don't let the fact that you are taking quicker steps force you to just run faster. Try to run at your normal training speed, but do it with a shorter, quicker stride rate. With some practice, you will soon find it becomes quite natural, and probably more comfortable.

and longer races relying more heavily on threshold training as the season comes to a close.

In addition, how many weeks are set aside for how many phases of training are a function of how long the season is. It may be that there is only enough time to have three phases, and even then the phases may be only four weeks each instead of the preferred six. One final note. You should always concentrate on your strengths late in the season. Work on your weaknesses early on.

Training Programs

Training for the 5K through 15K

Racing the 5K through 15K distances can be acutely painful. To prepare for these distances, you must train your aerobic capacity and lactate threshold to their maximum capabilities. This means solid foundation work, a strong emphasis on interval training, and enough time spent on repetitions and threshold runs that speeds close to your aerobic capacity become pleasant—or acceptable, at worst.

Phase I training—weeks 1-6 in a 24-week program—is the same for runners preparing for any race distance, at least regarding the type of running you need to do. Phase I is for easy running, stretching, strengthening exercises, and for getting back into the habit of regular, daily training. I prescribe nothing but steady, easy running for the first three weeks of Phase I. Weeks 4-6 can have a longer run and some strides thrown into the weekly plan. Remember, you shouldn't increase mileage more often than every third week and a long (L) run shouldn't be more than 25% of the week's total mileage.

The early-quality Phase II (weeks 7-12) program is a time for adjusting to quality running. Repetition (R) workouts are

5K to 15K

Week	Day 1	Day 2	Day 3	Day 4	Day 5	Day 6	Day 7
1-3	E	E	E	E	E	E	E
4-6	L	E/s	E/s	E	E	E/s	E/s
7	L/s	E	R-1	Ti*	E	E	I-1
8	L/s	E	E/s	R-2	E	E	I-1
9	L/s	E	R-1	Ti*	E	E	I-2/s
10	L/s	E	E/s	R-2	E	E	I-1
11	L/s	E	R-1	Ti*	E	E	I-2/s
12	L/s	E	E/s	R-2	E	E	I-1
13	L/s	E	I-1	T*	E	E	I or Race
14	L/s	E	I-1	Ti*	E	E	I or Race
15	L/s	E	I-1	T*	E	E	I or Race
16	L/s	E	I-1	Ti*	E	E	I or Race
17	L/s	E	I-1	T*	E	E	I or Race
18	L/s	E	I-1	Ti*	E	E	I or Race
19	L/s	E	T*	Mix	E	E	Race or I-1
20	L/s	E	Ti*	Mix	E	E	Race or I-2
21	L/s	E	T*	E	E	E	Race or I-1
22	L/s	E	Ti*	M or E	E	E	Race or Mix
23	L/s	E	T*	M or E	E	E	Race or Mix
24	L/s	E	Ti*	E	E	E	Race

Workout Description

E Comfortable running with good light turnover and rhythmic breathing. Amount of running is flexible—do enough to reach week's goal. Can be one or two runs or no run if you feel you need complete rest.

L **Weeks 1-6:** Up to 25% of week's total mileage

Weeks 7-12: Up to 25% of week's mileage or 15 miles (whichever is less), plus some strides in middle or at end of the run

Weeks 13-18: Up to 25% week's mileage or 2 hrs (whichever is less)

Weeks 19-24: Should decrease distance to 20% of week's mileage+4 strides

s Strides. **Weeks 1-12:** 5-6x20- to 30-second runs at comfortably-fast pace using light quick turnover (do not sprint these)

Weeks 13-24: 5-6x20- to 30-sec runs with 1-min rests at about mile pace

T* Steady 20-minute tempo run at **T**-pace, plus 4x200 Repetitions (**R**-pace)

Ti* **Weeks 7-12:** Sets of repeated miles at **T**-pace with 1-minute rests, up to 8% of week's total mileage or 10K (whichever is less)

Weeks 13-18: Repeated runs of 1 mile to 15 min each at **T**-pace with 1-min rests, up to 10% of week's mileage or 8 miles (whichever is less) + 4 strides

Weeks 19-24: Repeated 1000s, 1200s, or miles at **T**-pace with 2-min rests, up to 8% of week's mileage or 10K (whichever is less)

I Do either **I-1** or **I-2** + 4-6x200 **R**, up to 6% of wk's miles or 8K (whichever is less)

I-1 **Weeks 7-12:** Sets of 2 minutes hard + 1 minute easy + 1 minute hard + 30 seconds easy + 30 seconds hard + 30 seconds easy, up to 8% of week's mileage or 10K (whichever is less)

Weeks 13-18: Repeated 1000s, 1200s, or miles to suit ability (4-5 minutes per run) with 3- to 4-minute jog recoveries, up to 8% of week's total mileage or 10K (whichever is less)

Weeks 19-24: Sets of 2 minutes hard + 1 minute easy + 1 minute hard + 30 seconds easy + 30 seconds hard + 30 seconds easy, up to 6% of week's mileage or 5K (whichever is less), plus 4x200 **R**

I-2 **Weeks 7-12:** Sets of 4-minutes hard, 3-minutes easy, up to 8% of week's mileage or 10K (whichever is less)

Weeks 19-24: Sets of 3-minutes hard, 2-minutes easy, up to 6% of week's mileage, plus 4x200 **R**

R-1 Sets of 2x200 + 1x400 at **R**-pace, up to 5% of week's mileage (may be hills)

R-2 **Weeks 7-12:** Repeat 400s at **R**-pace, up to 5% of week's miles (may be hills)

Mix 2-4x1000 to 1-mile **T** + 2x1000-1200 **I** + 4x200 **R**, or 3-4x1000 **T** + 6x200 **R** + 2-mile acceleration: Each 400 should be 5 seconds faster than previous, with final 400 at about 3-K pace

Note: All **R** workouts are to be done with full recoveries between the individual runs.

important because they will allow an adjustment to faster running. But with full recoveries between quality runs in a workout, reps feel relatively comfortable, while they work on good, light, and quick leg turnover. Increase weekly mileage up to 10 miles, but only every third week. Threshold (T) runs are introduced, immediately following days of reps, and nonstructured interval (I) sessions are added at the end of each week. An occasional race can replace the week-end I session.

Phase III, weeks 13-18, is the most stressful phase of a medium-distance runner's program. It is possible to increase weekly mileage slightly (every third week), but mileage is not the main stress during this phase. The main emphasis is on long intervals (I training). Threshold (T) training also receives a fair amount of emphasis during this phase, both the steady, tempo run and longer sets of cruise intervals.

Phase IV—weeks 19-24—is the final phase of the season's program and should be viewed as a high performance phase. Clearly, the toughest days should be races, not training sessions. The long runs become a little less long, and the quality sessions become a little less strenuous. The long-interval workouts of Phase III are dropped completely, although some less structured intervals should be done during non-race weeks. Usually, runners who have reached more than 50 miles per week will benefit from cutting back by about 20%, but those who have not reached the 50-mile total can usually stay at their current load and do just fine.

Training for the Marathon

What separates longer distance races from shorter distances is that the bulk of a longer race is performed below the individual's lactate threshold. Instead, longer races place a considerable demand on carbohydrate fuel supply, body temperature mechanisms, and maintenance of adequate body fluids, all of which can affect race performance. On page 18 I present a "typical" marathon approach. Daniels' Running Formula contains two other programs that can be modified to fit your individual circumstances.

Phase I of a marathon program can often last longer than the usual six weeks. This is because some marathoners want to spend a long period of time building up mileage before launching into quality training. If it hasn't been long since you performed serious training, then six weeks is adequate for Phase I. But if you are training after a long layoff, or training for your first marathon, you may want to spend as much as two or three months just running and building up mileage to a point where you feel that you have a solid base. The emphasis here is on steady, easy (E) running and with some runs of an hour or more. The second half of Phase I should incorporate one long (L) run each week. Again, don't add more than 10 miles every third week when building up mileage.

It is during Phase II of a long-distance program that you prepare the body for the most strenuous Phase III training that is ahead. This means adding some quality sessions, such as threshold (T) runs and some intervals (I), to the previous steady, easy runs that made up Phase I. Many runners like to include hill running in their marathon buildup, and this is the phase where that fits best. However, formal rep (R) training is

Marathon

Week	Day 1	Day 2	Day 3	Day 4	Day 5	Day 6	Day 7
1-3	E	E	E	E	E	E	E
4-6	L	E/s	E/s	E	E	E/s	E/s
7 (.80P)	L	E/s	E/s	E	I-2	E/s	E
8 (.80P)	T-1	E/s	E	I-2	E/s	E/s	E
9 (.70P)	TL-1	E	E	E/s	I-1	E	E/s
10 (.90P)	L	E/s	E	I-1	E/s	E	E
11 (.90P)	TL-2	E	E/s	I-3	E	E	L
12 (.70P)	E/s	T-2	E	E/s	I-1	E	E
13 (1.00P)	L	E/s	E	Ti-1	E/s	E	E
14 (.90P)	TLT-1	E/s	E	E	Ti-2/s	E	E
15 (.80P)	MP-1	E/s	E	E	Ti-3/s	E	E
16 (1.00P)	L	E/s	E	T*	E/s	E	E
17 (.90P)	TLT-2	E/s	E	E	Ti-4/s	E	E
18 (.70P)	MP	E/s	E	E	Ti-1/s	E	E
19 (1.00P)	L-1	E	E	E	T-1	E	E
20 (.80P)	TLT	E	E	E	T*	E	E
21 (.70P)	L-1	E	E	T-2	E	E	E
22 (.70P)	MP	E	E	E	Ti-1	E	E
23 (.60P)	TL	E-1	E-2	E-2	Ti-2	E-3	E-3
24 (.40P)	L-2	E-4	T-3	E-4	E-2	E-5	E-5

NOTE: The P value under each numbered week of training refers to the amount of mileage for that coming week. A peak amount of weekly mileage for the season must first be established. The decimal portion of that peak is then set for the week in question. For example, if 100 miles will be the greatest (peak) mileage for any week this season, then .90P=.90x100=90 miles for that week. Start with a reasonable amount of running and follow mileage rules when increasing total distance.

Workout Description

E — Comfortable running with good light turnover and rhythmic breathing. Amount of running is flexible—do enough to reach week's goal. Can be one or two runs or no run if you feel you need complete rest.

E-1 — 14% of week's total mileage

E-2 — 10-12% of week's total mileage

E-3 — 10-15% of week's total mileage

E-4 — 16% of week's total mileage

E-5 — 20- to 30-minute easy run (may take one day off if travel to race interrupts)

L — **Weeks 1-6:** Up to 25% of week's total mileage
Weeks 7-18: Up to 25% of wk's mileage or 2 -1/2 hrs (whichever is less)

L-1 — Lesser of 22 miles or 2-1/2 hours

L-2 — Lesser of 15 miles or 2 hours

s — Strides. 5-6x20- to 30-sec runs at comfortably-fast pace (do not sprint these)

MP — Lesser of 15 miles or 2 hours at **MP** (projected marathon race pace)

MP-1 — Lesser of 12 miles or 1-2/3 hours at **MP**

T* — **Weeks 13-18:** 20-minute **T**, 10-minute jog, 20-minute **T**
Weeks 19-24: 1-hour **E**, 6x5- to 6-minute **T**, 15-minute **E**

T-1 — **Weeks 7-18:** Steady 20-minute tempo run at **T**-pace + 5-6 strides
Weeks 19-24: 35- to 40-minute **E** and 15- to 20-minute **T** done twice

T-2 — **Weeks 7-18:** 6 sets of 5- to 6-minute runs at **T**-pace with 1-minute rests
Weeks 19-24: 35- to 40-minute **E** and 15- to 20-minute **T** done twice

T-3 — 4x4-minute **T** with full recoveries

Ti-1 — 4x10- to 12-minute **T** with 2-minute recoveries

Ti-2 — **Weeks 13-18:** 4x5- to 6-minute **T** with 1-minute recoveries + 5 minutes rest + 3x5- to 6-minute **T** with 1-minute rests
Weeks 19-24: 3x10- to 12-minute **T** with 2-minute rests

Ti-3 — 15- to 20-minute **T** + 3 minutes rest + 15- to 20-minute **T** + 3 minutes rest + 10- to 12-minute **T** + 3 minutes rest + 15- to 20-minute **T**

Ti-4 — 8x5- to 6-minute **T** with 30-second rests

Workout Description

TL   2x10- to 15-minute **T** + 5-7 miles **E**

TL-1 5x5- to 6-minute **T** with 1-minute rests + 1-hour easy run

TL-2 2x10- to 12-minute **T** with 2-minute rests + 1-hour easy run

TLT 4x5- to 6-minute **T** with 1-minute rests + lesser of 10 miles or 80-minute **E** + 4x5- to 6-minute **T** with 1-minute rests

TLT-1 4x5- to 6-minute **T** with 1-minute rests + 1-hour **E** + 15- to 20-minute steady **T** pace

TLT-2 2x10- to 12-minute **T** with 2-minute rests + lesser of 10 miles or 80-minute **E** + 15- to 20-minute **T**

I-1   Sets of 1000s, 1200s, or miles at I-pace with 3- to 5-minute easy runs to recover, up to 8% of week's mileage or 10K (whichever is less)

I-2   Sets of 4 minutes hard + 3 minutes easy, up to 8% of week's mileage or 10K (whichever is less). *Note:* The word "hard" in **I** workouts means about 5K race pace, not faster

I-3   Sets of 5 minutes hard + 3-5 minutes easy, up to 8% of week's mileage or 10K (whichever is less)

not part of this program, which means that strides are the fastest running you will do. Hill training will have to be accomplished as part of interval sessions or incorporated into some of the longer runs.

Phase III consists of longer threshold (T) workouts, marathon-pace (MP) runs, and long runs that involve some threshold-pace running. Each week will generally consist of two or three quality sessions, and the remaining days will be easy (E) running.

Phase IV is the final-quality phase, and although similar in structure to Phase III, it should be less stressful since your mileage is coming down and you are becoming accustomed to the training. You should be tapering during the final two weeks leading to the marathon. This means your mileage should decrease, and the intensity of your runs should also decrease.

Jack Daniels has been head cross country coach for both men and women at the State University of New York at Cortland since 1986. Under his guidance, Cortland runners have won eight NCAA Division III National Championships. Called "The World's Greatest Running Coach" by *Runner's World* magazine, Daniels has advised some of America's finest runners, including Jim Ryun, Alberto Salazar, Joan Benoit Samuelson, Lisa Martin, Ken Martin, and Jerry Lawson. His latest book, *Daniels' Running Formula*, upon which this article is based, distills 40 years of thought, experience, and research into easily understood training principles and programs. To obtain a copy, please visit your local bookstore or contact the publisher, Human Kinetics, at 1.800.747.4457. ($16.95 plus S/H)

The aid station at the 23 mile mark was manned by a group
from the local junior high school... needless to say,
the fast approaching runners were not amused.

Using the Beat of Your Heart

There is no one-size-fits-all universal training program, for runners or for any other sports participant. Rather, exercise must be individually tailored to fit you. And that's just what heart zone training provides—a completely personalized exercise program that works for all people and all activities. It works for a 55-year-old professional athlete like me, a 60-year old with a family history of heart problems, a 70-year old wanting to improve strength, or an 80-year old who wants to climb to the third floor of a building without puffing. It works for a 20-year old who never was fit, a 30-year old who has become more sedentary from too much time in front of a computer, and a 40-year old who wants to get back to fitness again. It's a one-program-fits-all hearts way toward wellness.

Let's take heart zone training one part at a time by looking at those three words: Heart, Zone, and Training.

Heart. That's easy. Your heart's a muscle. It's a use-it-or-lose-it muscle so if you don't do cardiovascular exercise, you'll lose some of the heart's functional ability. It's the most important muscle in your entire body. It should be treated that way.

Zone. A zone is simply a range of heart beats. Recent research has shown powerful benefits from exercising in several different zones rather than one target zone to get maximum benefit in the least amount of time.

Training. Training is the regimen of exercising to achieve a goal. It's different than exercising. When you exercise you are doing it for the joy and benefit of the exercise. When you train, you want to accomplish a goal like get fitter, improve your health, or lower your blood pressure.

You can train smarter and get more benefits if and when you start using the beat of your heart.

Rating Your Heart Rate

Heart rate is a measurement tool to help in determining the health of your heart. The index is beats per minute (bpm). Some heart rate numbers are better than others. For example, you want to have a low resting heart rate measurement. You want to have high heart rate numbers if you are training hard, and you want to know what your sustainable heart rate values are as well. You have a maximum heart rate and an anaerobic threshold number. There are ways of measuring these values accurately and continuously, and to do so we use a heart rate monitor.

The tests to determine how fit your heart muscle is are relatively easy, and they don't take a lot of time. After taking some of them you'll want to re-test yourself to see if your training program is getting you cardiovascularly fitter. If you ever see wall charts about heart rate, especially the ones that set your heart zones for you, be cautious. They are assuming that you are "typical" or average, and few of us fit that category.

Determining Your Sport Specific Max Heart Rate

Remember: Before you take these tests, you should consult your physician to make sure you can do so safely.

Maximum heart rate can be determined in two ways: going to max or going to sub-max and predicting maximum. The arithmetic formulas (such as 220 bpm minus your age) are simply inaccurate. They are so inaccurate that you should not use one. Rather, take one of these two tests to determine your max.

Sub Max Walking Test. Go to a high school or college track and walk fast for four laps (usually one mile). Don't use a "race-walking" technique—just your normal comfortable walking style. During the last lap look at your monitor and take the average heart rate for that one lap. To determine your estimated maximum heart rate, add to this average last-lap heart rate the number that best matches your current fitness level as follows:

If you are in poor shape add 40 bpm
If you are in average shape add 50 bpm
If you are in excellent shape add 60 bpm

Max Heart Rate Run Test. Warm up adequately. Then starting at 125 bpm increase your running speed every 15 seconds by 5 bpm. Continue this until you are at maximum speed and can not continue to increase the speed. The highest number on your monitor is very, very close to your true maximum heart rate.

The Five Heart Zones

Heart zones are all expressed as a percentage of your maximum heart rate (MaxHR). They reflect exercise intensity. By training in each of the five different zones you'll realize five different results. Using your heart beat, you'll set each of these zones at 10% increments of your MaxHR.

The Five Heart Rate Zones

ZONE	% OF MAX HR	BENEFIT	EXERCISE EXAMPLE
REDLINE	100-90%	Improves performance	running very fast
ANAEROBIC (THRESHOLD)	90-80%	Improves endurance	running hard
AEROBIC	80-70%	Enhances cardio strength	running easily
TEMPERATE	70-60%	Burns high % of fat	jogging easily
HEALTHY HEART	60-50%	Strengthens your heart	walking briskly

The above chart illustrates the five heart rate zones. You should train on different days in one or more of the five different heart zones. This is called "time in zone" training, and here's what happens in each of them.

Zone 1 The Healthy Heart Zone: 50%–60% of your individual MaxHR

This is the safest, most comfortable zone, reached by walking briskly, swimming easily, doing any low intensity activity including mowing your lawn. Here you strengthen your heart and improve muscle mass while you reduce body fat, cholesterol, blood pressure, and your risk for degenerative disease. You get healthier in this zone, but not more aerobically fit—that is, it won't increase your endurance or strength but it will improve your health.

Zone 2 The Temperate Zone: 60%–70% of your individual MaxHR

It's easily reached by going a little faster like increasing from a walk to a jog. While still a relatively low level of effort, this zone starts training your body to increase the rate of fat release from the cells to the muscles for fuel. Some people have erroneously called this the "fat burning zone" because up to 85% of the total calories burned in this zone are fat calories. We actually burn fat in all zones.

Zone 3 The Aerobic Zone: 70%–80% of your individual MaxHR

In this zone—reached by running moderately—you improve your functional capacity. The number and size of your blood vessels actually increase, your lung capacity and respiratory rate improves, and your heart increases in size and strength so you can exercise longer before becoming fatigued. You're still metabolizing fats and carbohydrates but the ratio has changed—about a 50–50 rate, which means you are burning both equally.

Zone 4 The Anaerobic Threshold Zone: 80%–90% of your individual MaxHR

This zone is reached by going hard—running faster. Here you get faster and fitter, increasing your heart rate as you cross from aerobic to anaerobic training. At this point, your heart cannot pump enough blood and oxygen to supply the exercising muscles fully so they respond by continuing to contract anaerobically (this means without sufficient oxygen). This is where you "feel the burn." You can stay in this zone for a limited amount of time, usually not more than an hour. That's because the muscles just cannot sustain working anaerobically without fatiguing. The working muscles protect themselves from overwork by not being able to maintain the intensity level.

Zone 5 The Redline Zone: 90%–100% of your individual MaxHR

This is the equivalent of running very hard and is used mostly as an "interval" training regimen—exertion done only in short to intermediate length bursts. Even world-class athletes can stay in this zone for only a few minutes at a time. It's not a zone most people will select for exercising since working out here hurts. There is also an increased potential for injury, but you burn lots of calories, mostly carbohydrates.

The Training Tree

Now you understand that we use the beat of our heart as the source for determining how hard we exercise. Most people have been using how they feel, or they might use how fast they ride or run. With the technology of a heart rate monitor, you don't have to guess any longer, but rather you can train precisely. To do this we use the analogy of climbing up a tree called the Training Tree.

You go up and down the limbs of your new exercise tree, depending on your goals, at your own speed. As you climb the branches, you'll increase your all-around fitness, and your body will experience wonderful, truly incredible changes. The different training limbs like the different heart zones are based on the benefits you receive when you are training on that limb. From top to bottom they are as follows: base branch, endurance branch, speed branch, peak branch, racing branch (and of course the recovery trunk).

My book's *Heart Zone Training,* and *SMART HEART, High Performance Heart Zone Training*, each give you a number of sample training programs for each branch. *SMART HEART* also describes how to maintain a personal heart zone log, which *The Ultimate Runner's Journal* is perfectly suited for, to record your training in various zones to evaluate your total effort over a period of time.

The Training Tree

RACE

Choose this branch if you are training for competition.

PEAK

Choose this branch if you are preparing to race.

INTERVAL

Choose this branch if you are training to increase your speed.

STRENGTH

Choose this branch if you are training to be stronger.

ENDURANCE

Choose this branch if you are training your cardiovascular capacity.

BASE

Choose this branch if you are just starting to exercise.

RECOVERY

Choose the trunk if you are recuperating from an injury or you have overtrained.

Time In Zone, The TIZ System

What's great about the heart zone training program for runners is that it will work regardless of how much training time you have. By putting your training time into different zones you'll get fitter because you'll be varying your exercise intensity. The minimum training time for improvement has been an impossible number for exercise scientists to realize. If you forced an answer out of us, we'd agree that there is a minimum and there's a maximum but it's so individual for each person that it can't be generalized. Let's just say that 30 minutes 4 to 5 times a week, or a total training time of 120 to 150 minutes per week, can get you fit and keep you fit.

Once you have made a commitment to training time, you need to fit it into the different zones based on what branch of the training tree you are currently training within. The Time in Zone Tree on page 25 shows you how to take the total time and put it into the zones.

Setting Your Goals

This may be one of the most difficult steps to setting up your heart zone training program. There are two types of goals—short term and long term—both are key to improving. Just remember that all goals must fit the parameters of the word SMART which stands for specific, measurable, attainable, realistic, and timely. Spend some thoughtful time here and write them down in the front of *The Ultimate Runner's Journal* so you frequently see them.

Time In Zone Tree

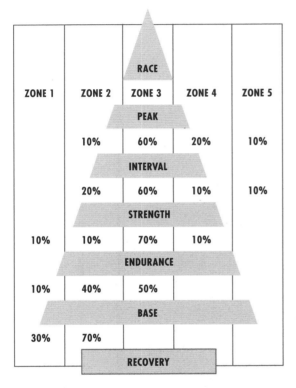

ZONE 1	ZONE 2	ZONE 3	ZONE 4	ZONE 5
		RACE		
		PEAK		
	10%	60%	20%	10%
		INTERVAL		
	20%	60%	10%	10%
		STRENGTH		
10%	10%	70%	10%	
		ENDURANCE		
10%	40%	50%		
		BASE		
30%	70%			
		RECOVERY		

The Steps to Heat Zone Training

Putting it all together is a step-by-step progression now that you have all of the parts to heart zone training for runners. Follow these steps and you'll have a program that works for a lifetime.

1. Determine your maximum heart rate
2. Set your five heart zone training zones (Z1 – Z5)
3. Set your short and long term training goals
4. Pick your current training tree branch
5. Set your weekly training time
6. Calculate your Time in Zone (TIZ)
7. Do your workouts
8. Fill in *The Ultimate Runner's Journal*
9. Complete monthly heart rate self-tests

Running must fit you as an individual. I'm convinced, and so are thousands of others who train using this technological approach, that it will lead to an integration of your mind, your body, and your spirit into a wellness exercise program that works. You'll begin to see positive benefits as you feel more energy and sleep better. I predict you'll also feel a real boost to your self-esteem that will make it fun to keep going.

Her latest book, *Fit and Fat: An 8-Week Heart Zones Training Program* is available in bookstores nationwide, and on the Heart Zones website, or by calling 916.481.7283.

She resides in Sacramento, California and Seattle, Washington.

Sally Edwards just turned 56 and is as passionate today about exercise as she was when she started thirty-five years ago. She practices what she preaches and has held world records in running, triathlons, snowshoeing, and extreme sport races.

In 1984 she ran in America's first Olympic Marathon Trials. Ten years later she set the woman's record for the Iditashoe, a 100-mile snowshoe event in Alaska. In 1995 and again in 1996 she participated in the 370-mile Eco Challenge adventure race. In October 2000, she finished her 16th Ironman Triathlon in Hawaii that includes a 2.4-mile swim, 112 miles by bike, and then a full 26.2-mile marathon. In September 2003, she again volunteered to finish last in her 94th consecutive Danskin Triathlon, every one since the series began.

Edwards holds a graduate degree in exercise physiology from Berkeley and a masters degree in business. She has authored 18 books and is noted for her inspirational public speaking and support of charitable concerns, especially The Susan G. Komen Breast Cancer Foundation.

"Son, this is known as a triathlon...
a race involving swimming, cycling and running.
However, today many of these athletes will not
be competing in the latter two events."

With only one port-o-hydrant available and the start
just moments away, things began to get
a little heated in the doggie line.

Nutrition and Athletic Performance

by Mary Coordt

Most people realize that their food habits can affect their health. In active people, diet can affect both health and athletic performance. Seems simple enough, but even the most dedicated runners can affect their performance by not eating properly. A runner's specific caloric and nutrient needs depend on many factors including gender, body size and training program. Since eating for energy is of the utmost importance for athletes, it is important to consider the energy-yielding nutrients (carbohydrates, protein and fat), in your everyday diet. Although making wise food choices will not guarantee a spot on an Olympic team, what and when you eat has a powerful influence on maximizing your running potential.

Energy Nutrients

In general, a diet that is high in carbohydrate (60 to 65 percent of total calories), low in fat (20 to 30 percent), and adequate in protein (12 to 15 percent) can be obtained by choosing a variety of nutrient-dense foods (foods that supply adequate vitamins and minerals for the energy they provide). Research clearly shows that a high carbohydrate diet can improve endurance. The body constantly uses and replenishes its glycogen, the storage form of glucose and the major fuel for exercise. Carbohydrate intake influences how much glycogen is stored, which in turn influences performance. Keep in mind that neither fat nor protein can restore glycogen. Most runners choose the same carbohydrates every day and miss out on important nutrients. Do your carbohydrates consist of crackers, pretzels, white breads, and plain pasta? By including a variety of whole grains, fruits, and vegetables, you will be supplied with the vitamin B6, zinc and antioxidants that many runners neglect.

Yes, nutrient-dense carbohydrates should make up the core of your diet, but this does not mean to neglect protein and fats! Many runners assume they need only carbohydrates and neglect protein, which is vital to the muscle repair process. Lean meats, fish, dairy and legumes are all good sources of protein to include in your diet.

Do you tend to avoid fat whenever you can in an attempt to become leaner and faster? Although that notion has some merit, many overdo it. It is true that heart disease is the nation's number one killer of adults and excess dietary fat (>30% total calorie intake) increases the risk for this disease. But be careful not to lower your fat intake too much. Recent research indicates that athletes on extremely low fat diets (<20 percent of total calories) have decreased endurance and muscle strength. So rather than thinking of fat as your enemy, select the essential, heart-healthy fats such as the ones found in fish, nuts, avocados and olive oil while limiting the amount of heart-damaging fats found in fried food and butter.

Eating Before a Run

Breakfast is essential! Yes, you *should* eat before your morning run or race. Keep in mind that we have limited stores of glycogen, so in the morning they are diminished from the overnight fast. Glycogen use depends on the intensity and duration of your exercise. The more strenuous the exercise, the faster your glycogen stores will be depleted. There are numerous studies that reveal that eating before a workout boosts endurance. Many people who eat breakfast report feeling better, with their perceived exertion significantly less compared to running on empty. So, fuel your muscles to ensure you have a strong run.

It is optimal to eat between two to four hours before a long run or race to allow the food time to be digested and nutrients to be absorbed. Choose high-carbohydrate, low fiber, low fat foods that are also moderate to low in protein to help speed digestion and avoid gastrointestinal (GI) distress. Depending on your body weight and workout, aim for 100 to 200 grams of carbohydrate, 400 to 800 calories to adequately generate glycogen to fuel your workout. If it is a shorter workout, you can experiment eating a smaller snack up to an hour before. Good choices include: bagels, toast with jam, bananas, cereal with low-fat milk or soymilk. For those who have trouble getting up early enough for breakfast, or can't tolerate eating in the morning, try experimenting with drinking some sports drink or a can of Ensure before a workout. If you are planning an easy, short run in the morning and insist on sleeping in until the last minute, a high-carbohydrate dinner the night before will be sufficient to get you through. In addition, drinking 16 ounces of water two hours before a race start will guarantee your fluid tanks are full and still leave enough time to "relieve yourself" of any excess.

Fueling During the Run

If your run will last longer than 90 minutes, it is important to fuel during the run. It is well documented that consuming carbohydrates during prolonged exercise (> 90 minutes) will enhance performance. Although it depends on the individual's glycogen storage and the intensity of the exercise, glycogen depletion occurs after 1 to 2 hours of running and will result in muscle fatigue. Without glucose to fuel muscles, the legs start to feel heavy and one cannot maintain running intensity. Marathon runners refer to this point of glucose exhaustion as "hitting the wall." Lack of glucose to the brain will cause weakness and lightheadedness, otherwise known as "bonking." To prevent these problems, be sure to consume 30 to 60 grams of carbohydrate an hour during your run.

In addition to the carbohydrate ingestion, remember to replace your fluid loss. Our sweat glands can produce up to two liters of sweat per hour (99% water) and if not replaced, you will experience a decrease in both cardiac output and blood flow to the muscles which can lead to a sub par performance. So, it is worth it to sacrifice a few seconds to stop at aid stations to replace fluid loss during a race. To avoid dehydration, drink 5 to 12 ounces of water every 15 to 20 minutes of exercise. Following are some ways to feed your brain and muscles so you don't "bonk" or "hit the wall!"

Sports drinks: Most are a combination of water, carbohydrates and some electrolytes such as sodium and potassium. The presence of small amounts of sodium helps the body retain fluids thereby maintaining plasma volume during activity and recovery. Select a flavor of sport drink you enjoy because you are more likely to drink it. Also, make sure the drink contains 6 to 9 percent carbohydrate which is the equivalent of 14 to 20 grams of carbohydrate per 8 ounce serving. This optimal amount facilitates gastric emptying and intestinal absorption making it more readily available to the exercising muscles. Drinks such as fruit juice, energy drinks and sodas provide too much carbohydrate so they are not as easily absorbed during strenuous exercise; furthermore, they can cause stomach upset. In ultra-endurance events, when the running intensity is not as demanding, many can tolerate de-fizzed cola and may benefit from the caffeine. During a training run, experiment several times to discover which drink works best for you.

Other products: If you are able to eat during a run, choose foods that meet the criteria described for pre-run meals — a high-carbohydrate source that is low in fat and protein in order to minimize GI distress. Pieces of a baked potato, a bagel, a banana, or pretzels are some foods many runners, especially ultra-endurance runners, snack on during long runs.

Sports bars are another option, but since the creation of the first high-carbohydrate bar made for athletes in the 1980s, they have been taken over by a 1.5 billion dollar a year industry that sells bars promising to cure all sorts of health problems. Striving to find a new niche, manufacturers compete to out-sell each other by claiming everything from "providing more energy", "building muscle", "help lose weight", to "making you smarter". Be certain to check the label and invest only in a bar that is intended to be eaten before or during exercise. Ideally, high-carbohydrate bars should supply 200 to 260 calories with greater than 70% of the calories from carbohydrates, no more than 15% of the calories from fat or protein and less than 5 to 6 grams of fiber. Some examples include Clif Bar, Power Bar and Gatorade Bar.

During more intense long runs, eating can be difficult. Therefore, sport gels may be worth trying. Sports gels can be easier on the GI tract and are an excellent way to quickly get 25 to 28 grams of carbohydrate and 100 calories. They also have the advantage of being light and portable. Many brands are available, including GU, Power Gel and Clif Shot. They come in a wide variety of flavors and some even come with caffeine.

Be sure to take the gel with 9 to 11 ounces of water for the most efficient absorption.

The Recovery

Your race or long run may be over, but your body is screaming for attention. A long or intense workout lasting over 60 to 90 minutes can leave you dehydrated and glycogen depleted. In other words, your gauge is on empty and if you do not refuel you will delay your recovery. What and when you eat after prolonged exercise is just as important as what you eat before or during a race.

The timing is as important as the composition of what you consume to initiate your recovery process. Several studies on runners and cyclists have repeatedly shown that consuming carbohydrates immediately after exercise versus two hours later can accelerate the rate of glycogen synthesis and expand muscle glycogen storage. Moreover, this practice resulted in a better performance during their next workout. Most athletes are not hungry after strenuous exercise and eating a potato or more pasta may not sound appealing. However, you may be thirsty and you do need fluids so by drinking a sport drink soon after crossing the finish line you can rehydrate and refuel at the same time. Replace each pound of body weight lost with 16 to 20 ounces of fluid. Drink beyond the feeling of thirst, as it is not a reliable indicator of hydration status.

While sport drinks are convenient, they are not sufficient for optimal recovery. Try to get some real food within the next 30 to 60 minutes. Several studies show that the combination of carbohydrate and protein, in a carbohydrate to protein ratio of 3 to 4:1, induces a faster rate of glycogen synthesis in the hours following exercise compared to either one given alone. In addition, including some protein in the post-race meal may aid in the muscle repair process. But do not over do it; excess protein in a post-race meal will not only impair glycogen synthesis, but it will slow digestion and absorption of the needed glucose from carbohydrates.

In addition, free radical formation increases after intense exercise. These free radicals are unstable, highly reactive substances that can damage muscle tissue and produce muscle soreness. Regular physical exercise increases your body's enzyme activity to help defend against the destructive nature of the free radicals. However, these enzymes cannot do the entire job. Antioxidants from your diet are needed to assist your defense system. Hence, it seems sensible to help fully protect yourself by consuming foods rich in antioxidants such as vitamin C, vitamin E and carotenoids. You have probably heard of beta-carotene, but there is a whole family of carotenes including lutein and lycopene. For foods that contain beta-carotene, look for brightly or deeply colored fruits and vegetables such as: carrots, peppers, sweet potatoes, kale, spinach, winter squash, mangos, and dried apricots. For foods rich in vitamin C, add bell peppers, tomatoes, strawberries and/or citrus fruit to your meals. And, incorporate more vitamin E in your diet with almonds, sunflower seeds, wheat germ, and leafy green vegetables.

A Few Diet Ideas:

Simple snack
- 3 ounces turkey breast on whole wheat bread, tomato & avocado
- 1 orange
- 2 oatmeal raisin cookies

The vegetarian
- Tofu stir-fry
- 1 cup sticky rice
- ½ cup tofu & vegetables (asparagus, kale, red bell pepper)
- 2 fortune cookies

Cool and soothing
- Smoothie (1 cup nonfat fruit yogurt, ½ cup blueberries, 1 cup strawberries, ½ cup mango, 1 cup soymilk, 2 teaspoons wheat germ)
- ½ cup of trail mix with almonds, sunflower seeds, dried apricots

Soup's on
- 2 cups chicken penne vegetable soup (green beans, tomatoes, peppers)
- 10 crackers
- 1 cup 1% milk
- 20 grapes

Hearty breakfast
- 1 waffle (7 inch) with 2 tablespoons maple syrup
- 2 ounces Canadian bacon
- 1 cup orange juice
- 1 large slice cantaloupe

5 Everyday Tips for Training Athletes

1. Eat quality protein. Endurance athletes need a bit more protein than a non-athlete (about 60 to 100 grams a day) that is easily met through lean meats, dairy, eggs and a variety of soy products.

2. Maintain your weight. As your weekly mileage and intensity increases, be cautious with calorie intake. Do not try to lose weight during the weeks of high volume training or strength and endurance will suffer. If one of your goals is to lose excess weight over a 6 month period...great! But during the critical training weeks, too many *already lean* athletes limit their food consumption in attempt to lose a few more pounds only to be disappointed when they get sick or struggle during workouts.

3. Maintain your fluid and electrolyte status. During prolonged endurance activity be sure to consume water, sports drinks and food to prevent dehydration and hyponatremia (low sodium in blood). Hyponatremia is a potentially dangerous condition that occurs when athletes neglect to replace electrolytes during events that take place in the heat or last longer than four hours.

4. Avoid anemia. Female athletes are at a high risk for iron deficiency anemia because of the blood loss from heavy menstrual bleeding, and lack of meat in their diet. Low iron stores will compromise oxygen delivery in the body and result in fatigue. However, there are many causes of anemia, so have your blood level tested to determine the specific cause. Do not self prescribe iron supplements. Rather, be smart and "beef up" your diet with the readily absorbable iron found in lean red meat and lesser amount found in poultry and fish. If you choose to avoid these richest sources, make sure to consume iron-fortified cereals with foods high in vitamin C (such as strawberries) to boost iron absorption from the less absorbable grain sources.

5. Become a nutrition skeptic! Don't fall prey to the nutrition fraud industry making over $25 billion a year. Research the product and make an informed decision. Although the internet can be a valuable source for accurate information, there are hundreds of millions of websites and the information is only as good as its source. Try to use directory sites of respected organizations, such as the American Medical Association (www.ama-assn.org), National Institute of Health (www.nih.gov), Food and Drug Administration (www.fda.gov), National Council Against Health Fraud (www.ncahf.org) rather than blind searches with a search engine that are rarely dependable.

Helpful Tips for a Healthier Athlete

Make smart choices when eating out

1. Choose grilled, steamed, or poached fish and meats rather than fried, sometimes called "crispy". And keep in mind one serving is 3 ounces, the size of a deck of cards.

2. Limit the amount of cheese on sandwiches, in salads and sauces.

3. Ask for condiments and dressings on the side.

4. Downsize rather than supersize. Most restaurant servings are 3 to 4 times larger than the recommended portions. Split a meal and add a salad or take home half for lunch the next day.

5. Think before you drink! Liquid calories don't trip our satiety mechanisms, so most people do not realize that these calories add on to the food calories. Liquid calories are a major contributor to the obesity epidemic. A 20 ounce soda is 250 calories; a 12 ounce beer is 150 calories; a Starbuck's

medium Tazoberry and cream packs 500 calories and 23 grams of fat; a 32 ounce Dunkin' Donuts Coolata means 740 calories and 32 grams of fat; even a small McDonalds' shake is 320 calories. While these are refreshing treats, they provide few nutrients for the calories they contribute. Even juices and smoothies can be calorie dense: Nantucket Nectars run around 300 calories for a bottle; Jamba Juice Strawberries Wild 32 ounce has 560 calories. Although juices and smoothies do provide some vitamins, you use up a significant amount of your daily calorie allotment. Drink unsweetened ice tea, water, or low-fat milk with the majority of your meals.

6. Never arrive at a restaurant starving or you will overeat. Snack on fruit, carrots or drink a glass of milk before leaving home.

7. Eat slow and enjoy your meal. This gives your body time for satiety to register, as well as being able to have a conversation with your company.

Healthful Hints for Eating at Home

1. To prevent impulse shopping, always shop from a list and on a FULL stomach!

2. Visualize your dinner plate! Prepare the meal so two-thirds consists of grains, legumes and vegetables and one-third is some type of meat or fish. This image will keep calories in control and provide fiber to keep you full.

3. Steam vegetables, and sauté foods in chicken or vegetable stock, wine, or water instead of fat.

4. Buy brown rice or other whole grains and add your own herbs and spices to provide flavor without the added fat; add in-season vegetables for additional nutrients and fiber.

5. Establish an "eating area" and require all meals take place there. This will discourage eating standing up and snacking in front of the TV.

6. Serve food in the kitchen and eat at the table so you are not tempted to keep adding to your plate during the meal from platters on the table. Do place the salad or vegetables on the table for seconds.

7. There are no prizes for finishing everything on your plate.

Mary Coordt earned a Masters of Science Degree in Nutrition from the University of California at Davis. Currently teaching nutrition courses in the Los Rios Community College district, Mary is a two-time U.S. Olympic Marathon Trials Qualifier (2000 and 2004). In her spare time, she enjoys presenting fundamental fitness and nutrition plans to many individuals and groups in her community. Mary resides in Elk Grove, California.

Accepting their coach's advice on the night before the big triathlon,
Cal, Hank and Mitch indulge in an evening of carbo-loading.

Calvin soon becomes the first marathoner to <u>literally</u> hit the wall at the 20-mile mark.

The 53 Runner's Commandments

by Joe Kelly

1. Don't be a whiner. Nobody likes a whiner, not even other whiners.
2. Walking out the door is often the toughest part of a run.
3. Don't make running your life. Make it part of your life.
4. During group training runs, don't let anyone run alone.
5. Keep promises, especially ones made to yourself.
6. When doing group runs, start on time no matter who's missing.
7. The faster you are the less you should talk about your times.
8. Keep a quarter in your pocket. One day you'll need to call for a ride.
9. Don't compare yourself to other runners.
10. All runners are equal, some are just faster than others.
11. Keep in mind that the later in the day it gets, the more likely it is that you won't run.
12. For a change of pace, get driven out and then run back.
13. If it was easy, everybody would be a runner.
14. When standing in starting lines, remind yourself how fortunate you are to be there.
15. Getting out of shape is much easier than getting into shape.
16. A bad day of running still beats a good day at work.
17. Talk like a runner. "Singlets" are worn on warm days. "Tank tops" are worn to the beach.
18. Don't talk about your running injuries. People don't want to hear about your sore knee or black toe.
19. Don't always run alone.
20. Don't always run with people.
21. Approach running as if the quality of your life depended on it.
22. No matter how slow you run it is still faster than someone sitting on a couch.
23. Keep in mind that the harder you run during training, the luckier you'll get during racing.
24. Races aren't just for those who can run fast.
25. There are no short cuts to running excellence.
26. The best runs sometimes come on days when you didn't feel like running.
27. Be modest after a race, especially if you have reason to brag.
28. If you say, "Let's run this race together," then you must stay with that person no matter how slow the pace.
29. Think twice before agreeing to run with someone during a race.
30. There is nothing boring about running. There are, however, boring people who run.
31. Look at hills as opportunities to pass people.
32. Distance running is like cod liver oil. At first it makes you feel awful, then it makes you feel better.
33. Never throw away the instructions to your running watch.
34. Don't try to outrun dogs.
35. Don't trust runners who show up at races claiming to be tired, out of shape or not feeling well. They get strong when the starter's gun goes off.
36. Don't wait for perfect weather. If you do, you won't run very often.

37. When tempted to stop being a runner, make a list of the reasons you started.
38. Never run alongside very old or very young racers. They get all the applause.
39. Without goals, training has no purpose.
40. During training runs, let the slowest runner in the group set the pace.
41. The first year in a new age group offers the best opportunity for trophies.
42. Go for broke, but be prepared to be broken.
43. Spend more time running on the roads than sitting on the couch.
44. Make progress in your training but progress at your own rate.
45. "Winning" means different things to different people.
46. Unless you make your living as a runner, don't take running too seriously.
47. Runners who never fail are runners who never try anything great.
48. Never tell a runner that he or she doesn't look good in tights.
49. Never confuse the Ben-Gay tube with the toothpaste tube.
50. Never apologize for doing the best you can.
51. Preventing running injuries is easier than curing them.
52. Running is simple. Don't make it complicated.
53. Running is always enjoyable. Sometimes, though, the joy doesn't come until the end of the run.

Joe Kelly is a marathon runner, an organizer of the Utica Boilermaker Road Race, and the director of the newly created National Distance Running Hall of Fame in Utica, New York. For many years he wrote magazine and newspaper columns, and he is the author of five books, including *Never Wear Black Socks Or A Plain White T-Shirt While Running*, from which these commandments were taken. To order an autographed copy of his book of running truths, send $8.95, plus $1.25 for shipping and handling, to Good Times Publishing, P.O. Box 4545, Utica, NY 13504. Quantity discounts are available. For more information, contact Kathy Kelly at 315.768.1730.

Runner's Log: A Runner's Retreat

by Tim Martin

Log Entry #1: The forest stretches from horizon to horizon, a carpet of green interlaced by ribbons of twisted silver streams. There are no signs of civilization. Nothing except wilderness. I have come here to connect with nature. To refresh the batteries of my tormented soul. To tap into some primitive side of myself, and purify my running.
I had no idea it would be so hard to get cable.

Log entry #2: I gave up my crowded urban existence filled with neurotic office workers, SUVs, Ginzu knives and CDs, and came here to run. I was croissanted-out. Filled with dot-coms. I was too busy to even make my meetings at Workaholics Anonymous. That is why I run on the shore of this lake, to detour from my sojourn through the so-called civilized life.
I miss the e-trading, though.

Log entry #3: I have kicked back with a vengeance. Nothing to do but run. Nothing at all. Wow. It's weird when there's nothing to do. I mean, here I am in the middle of nowhere. No worries. No care. I'm beginning to feel like my prehistoric ancestors. Moving through the forest, sleeping on the ground, my hair matted in crusty clumps. *What I wouldn't give for a shower about now.*

Log entry #4: Today I had a close encounter with the natural world. I ran around the lake and observed it with a strange luminescence in my eyes, something that seemed to transcend joy altogether and rise up into the realms of spiritual ecstasy. It burned through my soul like a hot rock. It was eating me alive.
I should have remembered the bug spray.

Log entry #5: Ran in the hills. Like a roving Bushman of the Kalahari I am in touch with all living things. Honing my senses in order to use nature's signs, rhythms, plants and energies to heal sickness and gain self-understanding and peace of mind. Every aspect of my being has been transformed. I have developed a new energy. An astonishing insight into the nature of reality.
I just wish there was a Starbucks somewhere nearby.

Log entry #6: I am in a primal zone, so deeply intoxicated that I attained a higher level of clarity. My ruminations and inspirations must have their birth in the clouds, in the ripples of the pond, and in the song of the distant sparrow. My hearing is alive with the song of the forest.
Especially since my Walkman went on the fritz.

Log entry #7: I adjust to my new surroundings as if I'd been born here. I have kinship with the earth, trees and shrubs. To put it another way, my mojo is working. Apparently, I have traveled beyond the area where bodily needs interject themselves. I am too busy to have a body. I am pure spirit. I am nothing but movement. I am a transparent vector for the will of my legs.
I'm thirsty, too. *What I wouldn't give for a brewski.*

Log entry #8: I heard water evaporate today. I listened to the tick of my own biology. I was reborn. I let it flow. I rolled with the punches. I allowed my mind to hitch a ride on whatever came through. I let go of my geo.
I had to. The payments were killing me.

Log entry #9: I am running in an entirely natural state now, grooving on sunshine, endorphins and wall calendar scenery. My line of sight is clear. I am in the zone, the zone is in me. I have channeled my aura. I have developed a mantra, a totemic word. I repeat it until it blocks out all other thoughts.

If this isn't a one-way ticket to a mental institution, I don't know what is.

Log entry #10: It is the eleventh hour of my eleventh day when I discover that I am sick of this place. No, I mean it. Really sick. I miss my toxin-, sugar-, starch-, glucose-, MSG-, dairy-, salt-, meat-, fur-, leather-, TV-, plastic-, Red Dye No. 2-, smoke-, noise-, A/C-, cell-phoning existence. I'd rather stick pins in my eyes than stay here another day. I head back to the city. I now understand this is the one place that will bring me peace, happiness and deep satisfaction.

So that's what I'm doing. Running down a smog-choked street, dodging cars, dogs, and pedestrians. And it feels right. It's in my blood now. It is my blood. I'm just kicking myself that I didn't think of this sooner.

Tim Martin is the author of *There's Nothing Funny About Running: Over 60 Wacky Short Stories on Running.* He has written for *Running Times, Marathon & Beyond,* and *City Sports Magazine.* In 1995, he was selected as Road Runners Club of America National Club Writer of the Year. He lives in the Pacific Northwest town of McKinleyville.

While expecting to experience a runner's high, Hank was quickly disappointed when he only received a simple runner's howdy.

PART II The Journal

How to Use the Journal

The Ultimate Runner's Journal log sheet to the right contains sample workout entries. The log sheets are easily modified to fit your own needs. Here is one way to chronicle your workouts:

First, fill in the week on the upper outside corner of the right-hand-page. This sample is taken from the week of May 5 to May 11. Enter the entry's date on the line to the right of the day of the week.

Every day before you run, write in the goal for that particular day's workout. Hopefully, you have a written training plan to meet your short-term and long-term goals. In the example to the right, you see goals for Friday, May 9, Saturday, May 10, and Sunday, May 11. After a workout, first enter the objective information pertaining to the workout. The given example utilizes all categories starting with route and then total elapsed distance, total elapsed time, type of workout completed (such as easy run, tempo, fartlek, intervals, long run, etc.), average heart rate, morning heart rate, the weather during the run, and any cross training performed that day.

In the Notes Section, you get specific about any aspect of your run or other workouts. For example, the May 9 entry contains splits for the five loops around the park and corresponding heart rates. Next comes a general statement of how you felt during that particular workout, and whether you met that day's goal. If you did not fulfill your goal for that day, indicate why you think you did not meet it. In other words, your excuse goes here. All of this information gives you valuable insights into how your training is progressing, and whether you need to make any adjustments. You will also find plenty of room to specify with whom you worked out, your topic of conversation, etc. The more information you jot down, the more fun you will have when looking back on your log in the future. Sometimes remembering a good run is almost as good as going on one.

At the end of each week, another notes section affords room for you to review your week of training, especially in relation to what you wanted to accomplish.

Goal Map

Starting on page 150 is a 52-week Goal Map. This is where you can, in one place, record your intended workout schedule for the day, week, or month, and then log what you actually did. The purpose of the Goal Map is to make it easy to identify any needed adjustment in your training.

Race Record

Pages 163 and 164 is the place to record your races for the year, with lots of space to write your comments or excuses.

Favorite Runs

We all have our favorite courses that we run over and over. Perhaps you like to do your 5-mile tempo runs in the park because each loop is exactly 2.5 miles. The Favorite Run tables on page 165 is where you can record these workouts in one place to chart your progression.

Unsolicited Advice

Finally, *The Ultimate Runner's Journal*, or any running log for that matter, should be a motivator and not a stress inducer. Having a training plan is extremely important, but remain flexible and use the most valuable training resource available – your own intuition. If your schedule calls for a difficult interval session and you are dead-dog tired, you probably should be flexible and bag it. Rest days or off days are just as important as your hard days. Enjoy and have fun with your training and results will follow.

Week 1

FRI | May 9
[date]

today's goal

7 miles
easy run

route	McKinley Park – Five Laps		distance	7 miles
notes	Warmup – 6:30; 8:10; 8:05; 8:08; 8:15; 8:11; Warndown – 6:05		time	53:24
	HR: 138; 145; 148; 149; 149; 150; 142		workout	Easy run
			heart rate	147 avg
	Nice and easy run with Brian. Still a bit tired from Wednesday's intervals, but		morning hr	50
	overall felt fine.		weather	warm, 82°
			x training	weights 1 hour

SAT | May 10
[date]

today's goal

15 mile
long run

route	Bike Trail – Nimbus to mile mark 30		distance	15 miles
notes	8:00; 8:02; 8:01; 8:05; 8:09; 8:02; 8:01; 8:03; 8:06; 8:09		time	2:01:23
	HR: 133; 137; 140; 141; 141; 145; 147; 147; 146; 148		workout	Long run
	8:05; 8:07; 8:13; 8:09; 8:11		heart rate	146 avg
	HR: 155; 148; 146; 149; 150		morning hr	52
	Great run with Leukemia Society. Felt ok, but left calf a little sore. Still cool in the		weather	70°-80°
	mornings.		x training	none

SUN | May 11
[date]

today's goal

Easy run

route	Generic loop along river		distance	6 miles
notes			time	49:12
	Ran the generic loop with Eric and Kathy.		workout	Easy run
	Talked about getting a team together for CIM relay.		heart rate	143 avg
			morning hr	53
	Left calf felt much better after I stretched and iced it yesterday.		weather	78°
			x training	crunches

NOTES

Overall was a very good week. I felt strong during my intervals and long run.
Accomplished all my goals. Training is going well. Should be ready
for the big race in December. Need to stretch more after I run though
because my left calf keeps acting up.
Next week I want to add a fartlek and do my long run at the
Auburn Overlook.

Distance for week	46 miles
Time for week	5:47:48
Distance to date	46 miles
End of week weight	not a chance
Total mileage on shoes	189 miles
End of week hr	53

The best time to start running was 20 years ago. The second best time is today.

Joe Kelly (American runner, writer & race organizer)

MON
[date]

today's goal

route |
notes |

distance |
time |
workout |
heart rate |
morning hr |
weather |
x training |

TUE
[date]

today's goal

route |
notes |

distance |
time |
workout |
heart rate |
morning hr |
weather |
x training |

WED
[date]

today's goal

route |
notes |

distance |
time |
workout |
heart rate |
morning hr |
weather |
x training |

THU
[date]

today's goal

route |
notes |

distance |
time |
workout |
heart rate |
morning hr |
weather |
x training |

Week   1

FRI

[date]

today's goal

route |
notes |

distance |
time |
workout |
heart rate |
morning hr |
weather |
x training |

SAT

[date]

today's goal

route |
notes |

distance |
time |
workout |
heart rate |
morning hr |
weather |
x training |

SUN

[date]

today's goal

route |
notes |

distance |
time |
workout |
heart rate |
morning hr |
weather |
x training |

NOTES

Distance for week
Time for week
Distance to date
End of week weight
Total mileage on shoes
End of week hr

The journey is just beginning.

Nena O'Neill & George O'Neill (American writers)

MON
[date]

today's goal

route | distance |
notes | time |
workout |
heart rate |
morning hr |
weather |
x training |

TUE
[date]

today's goal

route | distance |
notes | time |
workout |
heart rate |
morning hr |
weather |
x training |

WED
[date]

today's goal

route | distance |
notes | time |
workout |
heart rate |
morning hr |
weather |
x training |

THU
[date]

today's goal

route | distance |
notes | time |
workout |
heart rate |
morning hr |
weather |
x training |

Week 2

FRI
[date]

today's goal

route |
notes |

distance |
time |
workout |
heart rate |
morning hr |
weather |
x training |

SAT
[date]

today's goal

route |
notes |

distance |
time |
workout |
heart rate |
morning hr |
weather |
x training |

SUN
[date]

today's goal

route |
notes |

distance |
time |
workout |
heart rate |
morning hr |
weather |
x training |

NOTES

Distance for week
Time for week
Distance to date
End of week weight
Total mileage on shoes
End of week hr

I don't jog. If I die I want to be sick.

Abe Lemons

MON
[date]

today's goal

route	distance
notes	time
	workout
	heart rate
	morning hr
	weather
	x training

TUE
[date]

today's goal

route	distance
notes	time
	workout
	heart rate
	morning hr
	weather
	x training

WED
[date]

today's goal

route	distance
notes	time
	workout
	heart rate
	morning hr
	weather
	x training

THU
[date]

today's goal

route	distance
notes	time
	workout
	heart rate
	morning hr
	weather
	x training

Week ___ 3

FRI
[date]

today's goal

route |
notes |

distance |
time |
workout |
heart rate |
morning hr |
weather |
x training |

SAT
[date]

today's goal

route |
notes |

distance |
time |
workout |
heart rate |
morning hr |
weather |
x training |

SUN
[date]

today's goal

route |
notes |

distance |
time |
workout |
heart rate |
morning hr |
weather |
x training |

NOTES

Distance for week
Time for week
Distance to date
End of week weight
Total mileage on shoes
End of week hr

Workouts are like brushing my teeth; I don't think about them, I just do them.

PattiSue Plummer (American runner & Olympian)

MON
[date]

route | distance |
notes | time |

today's goal

workout |
heart rate |
morning hr |
weather |
x training |

TUE
[date]

route | distance |
notes | time |

today's goal

workout |
heart rate |
morning hr |
weather |
x training |

WED
[date]

route | distance |
notes | time |

today's goal

workout |
heart rate |
morning hr |
weather |
x training |

THU
[date]

route | distance |
notes | time |

today's goal

workout |
heart rate |
morning hr |
weather |
x training |

Week 4

FRI
[date]

today's goal

route
notes

distance
time
workout
heart rate
morning hr
weather
x training

SAT
[date]

today's goal

route
notes

distance
time
workout
heart rate
morning hr
weather
x training

SUN
[date]

today's goal

route
notes

distance
time
workout
heart rate
morning hr
weather
x training

NOTES

Distance for week
Time for week
Distance to date
End of week weight
Total mileage on shoes
End of week hr

My belly looked like a sack of Gummy Bears.

Writer Tim Martin on why he started running again

MON

[date]

today's goal

route

notes

distance

time

workout

heart rate

morning hr

weather

x training

TUE

[date]

today's goal

route

notes

distance

time

workout

heart rate

morning hr

weather

x training

WED

[date]

today's goal

route

notes

distance

time

workout

heart rate

morning hr

weather

x training

THU

[date]

today's goal

route

notes

distance

time

workout

heart rate

morning hr

weather

x training

Week **5**

[week of:]

FRI

[date]

today's goal

route
notes

distance
time
workout
heart rate
morning hr
weather
x training

SAT

[date]

today's goal

route
notes

distance
time
workout
heart rate
morning hr
weather
x training

SUN

[date]

today's goal

route
notes

distance
time
workout
heart rate
morning hr
weather
x training

NOTES

Distance for week
Time for week
Distance to date
End of week weight
Total mileage on shoes
End of week hr

Those who say it cannot be done should not interrupt those doing it.

Michael Johnson's trainer

MON
[date]

today's goal

route |
notes |

distance |
time |
workout |
heart rate |
morning hr |
weather |
x training |

TUE
[date]

today's goal

route |
notes |

distance |
time |
workout |
heart rate |
morning hr |
weather |
x training |

WED
[date]

today's goal

route |
notes |

distance |
time |
workout |
heart rate |
morning hr |
weather |
x training |

THU
[date]

today's goal

route |
notes |

distance |
time |
workout |
heart rate |
morning hr |
weather |
x training |

Week 6

FRI

[date]

today's goal

route |
notes |

distance |
time |
workout |
heart rate |
morning hr |
weather |
x training |

SAT

[date]

today's goal

route |
notes |

distance |
time |
workout |
heart rate |
morning hr |
weather |
x training |

SUN

[date]

today's goal

route |
notes |

distance |
time |
workout |
heart rate |
morning hr |
weather |
x training |

NOTES

Distance for week
Time for week
Distance to date
End of week weight
Total mileage on shoes
End of week hr

...Any day I am too busy to run is a day I am too busy.

John Bryant (Deputy Editor, London *Times*)

MON

[date]

route |
notes |

today's goal

distance |
time |
workout |
heart rate |
morning hr |
weather |
x training |

TUE

[date]

route |
notes |

today's goal

distance |
time |
workout |
heart rate |
morning hr |
weather |
x training |

WED

[date]

route |
notes |

today's goal

distance |
time |
workout |
heart rate |
morning hr |
weather |
x training |

THU

[date]

route |
notes |

today's goal

distance |
time |
workout |
heart rate |
morning hr |
weather |
x training |

Week ___ 7

FRI
[date]

today's goal

route |
notes |

distance |
time |
workout |
heart rate |
morning hr |
weather |
x training |

SAT
[date]

today's goal

route |
notes |

distance |
time |
workout |
heart rate |
morning hr |
weather |
x training |

SUN
[date]

today's goal

route |
notes |

distance |
time |
workout |
heart rate |
morning hr |
weather |
x training |

NOTES

Distance for week
Time for week
Distance to date
End of week weight
Total mileage on shoes
End of week hr

Winners don't do different things. Winners do things differently.

Anonymous

MON
[date]

today's goal

route |
notes |

distance |
time |
workout |
heart rate |
morning hr |
weather |
x training |

TUE
[date]

today's goal

route |
notes |

distance |
time |
workout |
heart rate |
morning hr |
weather |
x training |

WED
[date]

today's goal

route |
notes |

distance |
time |
workout |
heart rate |
morning hr |
weather |
x training |

THU
[date]

today's goal

route |
notes |

distance |
time |
workout |
heart rate |
morning hr |
weather |
x training |

Week   8

FRI
[date]

route |
notes |

today's goal

distance |
time |
workout |
heart rate |
morning hr |
weather |
x training |

SAT
[date]

route |
notes |

today's goal

distance |
time |
workout |
heart rate |
morning hr |
weather |
x training |

SUN
[date]

route |
notes |

today's goal

distance |
time |
workout |
heart rate |
morning hr |
weather |
x training |

NOTES

Distance for week
Time for week
Distance to date
End of week weight
Total mileage on shoes
End of week hr

Even if you're on the right track, you'll get run over if you just sit there.

Will Rogers (American humorist)

MON
[date]
today's goal

route		distance	
notes		time	
		workout	
		heart rate	
		morning hr	
		weather	
		x training	

TUE
[date]
today's goal

route		distance	
notes		time	
		workout	
		heart rate	
		morning hr	
		weather	
		x training	

WED
[date]
today's goal

route		distance	
notes		time	
		workout	
		heart rate	
		morning hr	
		weather	
		x training	

THU
[date]
today's goal

route		distance	
notes		time	
		workout	
		heart rate	
		morning hr	
		weather	
		x training	

Week 9

FRI
[date]

today's goal

route
notes

distance
time
workout
heart rate
morning hr
weather
x training

SAT
[date]

today's goal

route
notes

distance
time
workout
heart rate
morning hr
weather
x training

SUN
[date]

today's goal

route
notes

distance
time
workout
heart rate
morning hr
weather
x training

NOTES

Distance for week
Time for week
Distance to date
End of week weight
Total mileage on shoes
End of week hr

You must do the thing you think you cannot do.

Eleanor Roosevelt (American First Lady)

MON

[date]

today's goal

route	distance
notes	time
	workout
	heart rate
	morning hr
	weather
	x training

TUE

[date]

today's goal

route	distance
notes	time
	workout
	heart rate
	morning hr
	weather
	x training

WED

[date]

today's goal

route	distance
notes	time
	workout
	heart rate
	morning hr
	weather
	x training

THU

[date]

today's goal

route	distance
notes	time
	workout
	heart rate
	morning hr
	weather
	x training

Week 10

FRI
[date]

today's goal

route
notes

distance
time
workout
heart rate
morning hr
weather
x training

SAT
[date]

today's goal

route
notes

distance
time
workout
heart rate
morning hr
weather
x training

SUN
[date]

today's goal

route
notes

distance
time
workout
heart rate
morning hr
weather
x training

NOTES

Distance for week
Time for week
Distance to date
End of week weight
Total mileage on shoes
End of week hr

I don't drink. I don't kiss girls. These things do an athlete in.

Suleiman Nyambui (Tanzanian Olympic runner)

MON
[date]
route | distance |
notes | time |
today's goal
workout |
heart rate |
morning hr |
weather |
x training |

TUE
[date]
route | distance |
notes | time |
today's goal
workout |
heart rate |
morning hr |
weather |
x training |

WED
[date]
route | distance |
notes | time |
today's goal
workout |
heart rate |
morning hr |
weather |
x training |

THU
[date]
route | distance |
notes | time |
today's goal
workout |
heart rate |
morning hr |
weather |
x training |

Week 11

FRI
[date]

today's goal

route |
notes |

distance |
time |
workout |
heart rate |
morning hr |
weather |
x training |

SAT
[date]

today's goal

route |
notes |

distance |
time |
workout |
heart rate |
morning hr |
weather |
x training |

SUN
[date]

today's goal

route |
notes |

distance |
time |
workout |
heart rate |
morning hr |
weather |
x training |

NOTES

Distance for week
Time for week
Distance to date
End of week weight
Total mileage on shoes
End of week hr

We can't all be heroes because somebody has to sit on the curb and clap as they go by.

Will Rogers (American humorist)

MON
[date]

today's goal

route |
notes |

distance |
time |
workout |
heart rate |
morning hr |
weather |
x training |

TUE
[date]

today's goal

route |
notes |

distance |
time |
workout |
heart rate |
morning hr |
weather |
x training |

WED
[date]

today's goal

route |
notes |

distance |
time |
workout |
heart rate |
morning hr |
weather |
x training |

THU
[date]

today's goal

route |
notes |

distance |
time |
workout |
heart rate |
morning hr |
weather |
x training |

Week 12

FRI
[date]

today's goal

route |
notes |

distance |
time |
workout |
heart rate |
morning hr |
weather |
x training |

SAT
[date]

today's goal

route |
notes |

distance |
time |
workout |
heart rate |
morning hr |
weather |
x training |

SUN
[date]

today's goal

route |
notes |

distance |
time |
workout |
heart rate |
morning hr |
weather |
x training |

NOTES

Distance for week
Time for week
Distance to date
End of week weight
Total mileage on shoes
End of week hr

Good things come slow—especially in distance running.

Bill Dellinger (American track coach)

MON
[date]

today's goal

route | distance |
notes | time |
workout |
heart rate |
morning hr |
weather |
x training |

TUE
[date]

today's goal

route | distance |
notes | time |
workout |
heart rate |
morning hr |
weather |
x training |

WED
[date]

today's goal

route | distance |
notes | time |
workout |
heart rate |
morning hr |
weather |
x training |

THU
[date]

today's goal

route | distance |
notes | time |
workout |
heart rate |
morning hr |
weather |
x training |

Week ___ 13 ___

FRI

[date]

today's goal

route

notes

distance

time

workout

heart rate

morning hr

weather

x training

SAT

[date]

today's goal

route

notes

distance

time

workout

heart rate

morning hr

weather

x training

SUN

[date]

today's goal

route

notes

distance

time

workout

heart rate

morning hr

weather

x training

NOTES

Distance for week

Time for week

Distance to date

End of week weight

Total mileage on shoes

End of week hr

Run like hell and get the agony over with.

Clarence DeMar (7-Time Boston Marathon champion)

MON
[date]

route |
notes |

today's goal

distance |
time |
workout |
heart rate |
morning hr |
weather |
x training |

TUE
[date]

route |
notes |

today's goal

distance |
time |
workout |
heart rate |
morning hr |
weather |
x training |

WED
[date]

route |
notes |

today's goal

distance |
time |
workout |
heart rate |
morning hr |
weather |
x training |

THU
[date]

route |
notes |

today's goal

distance |
time |
workout |
heart rate |
morning hr |
weather |
x training |

Week 14

FRI

[date]

today's goal

route |
notes |

distance |
time |
workout |
heart rate |
morning hr |
weather |
x training |

SAT

[date]

today's goal

route |
notes |

distance |
time |
workout |
heart rate |
morning hr |
weather |
x training |

SUN

[date]

today's goal

route |
notes |

distance |
time |
workout |
heart rate |
morning hr |
weather |
x training |

NOTES

Distance for week
Time for week
Distance to date
End of week weight
Total mileage on shoes
End of week hr

There's no traffic jam on the extra mile.

Unknown

MON
[date]

today's goal

route

notes

distance

time

workout

heart rate

morning hr

weather

x training

TUE
[date]

today's goal

route

notes

distance

time

workout

heart rate

morning hr

weather

x training

WED
[date]

today's goal

route

notes

distance

time

workout

heart rate

morning hr

weather

x training

THU
[date]

today's goal

route

notes

distance

time

workout

heart rate

morning hr

weather

x training

Week 15

FRI

[date]

today's goal

route

notes

distance

time

workout

heart rate

morning hr

weather

x training

SAT

[date]

today's goal

route

notes

distance

time

workout

heart rate

morning hr

weather

x training

SUN

[date]

today's goal

route

notes

distance

time

workout

heart rate

morning hr

weather

x training

NOTES

Distance for week

Time for week

Distance to date

End of week weight

Total mileage on shoes

End of week hr

He who hesitates is a damn fool.

Mae West (American actress)

MON
[date]

today's goal

route
notes

distance
time
workout
heart rate
morning hr
weather
x training

TUE
[date]

today's goal

route
notes

distance
time
workout
heart rate
morning hr
weather
x training

WED
[date]

today's goal

route
notes

distance
time
workout
heart rate
morning hr
weather
x training

THU
[date]

today's goal

route
notes

distance
time
workout
heart rate
morning hr
weather
x training

Week ___ 16

FRI
[date]

today's goal

route |
notes |

distance |
time |
workout |
heart rate |
morning hr |
weather |
x training |

SAT
[date]

today's goal

route |
notes |

distance |
time |
workout |
heart rate |
morning hr |
weather |
x training |

SUN
[date]

today's goal

route |
notes |

distance |
time |
workout |
heart rate |
morning hr |
weather |
x training |

NOTES

Distance for week
Time for week
Distance to date
End of week weight
Total mileage on shoes
End of week hr

Running is my lover.

Toshihiko Seko (2-Time Boston Marathon champion)

MON
[date]

today's goal

route |
notes |

distance |
time |
workout |
heart rate |
morning hr |
weather |
x training |

TUE
[date]

today's goal

route |
notes |

distance |
time |
workout |
heart rate |
morning hr |
weather |
x training |

WED
[date]

today's goal

route |
notes |

distance |
time |
workout |
heart rate |
morning hr |
weather |
x training |

THU
[date]

today's goal

route |
notes |

distance |
time |
workout |
heart rate |
morning hr |
weather |
x training |

Week ____ 17 ──────

FRI _____
[date]

today's goal	route		distance	
	notes		time	
			workout	
			heart rate	
			morning hr	
			weather	
			x training	

SAT _____
[date]

today's goal	route		distance	
	notes		time	
			workout	
			heart rate	
			morning hr	
			weather	
			x training	

SUN _____
[date]

today's goal	route		distance	
	notes		time	
			workout	
			heart rate	
			morning hr	
			weather	
			x training	

NOTES

Distance for week

Time for week

Distance to date

End of week weight

Total mileage on shoes

End of week hr

Success is simply a matter of luck. Ask any failure.

Earl Wilson

MON

[date]

today's goal

route |
notes |

distance |
time |
workout |
heart rate |
morning hr |
weather |
x training |

TUE

[date]

today's goal

route |
notes |

distance |
time |
workout |
heart rate |
morning hr |
weather |
x training |

WED

[date]

today's goal

route |
notes |

distance |
time |
workout |
heart rate |
morning hr |
weather |
x training |

THU

[date]

today's goal

route |
notes |

distance |
time |
workout |
heart rate |
morning hr |
weather |
x training |

Week 18

FRI
[date]

today's goal

route
notes

distance
time
workout
heart rate
morning hr
weather
x training

SAT
[date]

today's goal

route
notes

distance
time
workout
heart rate
morning hr
weather
x training

SUN
[date]

today's goal

route
notes

distance
time
workout
heart rate
morning hr
weather
x training

NOTES

Distance for week
Time for week
Distance to date
End of week weight
Total mileage on shoes
End of week hr

The will to win means nothing without the will to prepare.

Juma Ikangaa (Tanzanian NYC Marathon champion)

MON
[date]

today's goal

route | distance |
notes | time |
    workout |
    heart rate |
    morning hr |
    weather |
    x training |

TUE
[date]

today's goal

route | distance |
notes | time |
    workout |
    heart rate |
    morning hr |
    weather |
    x training |

WED
[date]

today's goal

route | distance |
notes | time |
    workout |
    heart rate |
    morning hr |
    weather |
    x training |

THU
[date]

today's goal

route | distance |
notes | time |
    workout |
    heart rate |
    morning hr |
    weather |
    x training |

Week 19

FRI

[date]

today's goal

route

notes

distance

time

workout

heart rate

morning hr

weather

x training

SAT

[date]

today's goal

route

notes

distance

time

workout

heart rate

morning hr

weather

x training

SUN

[date]

today's goal

route

notes

distance

time

workout

heart rate

morning hr

weather

x training

NOTES

Distance for week

Time for week

Distance to date

End of week weight

Total mileage on shoes

End of week hr

Failure is not failure but the opportunity to begin again...more intelligently.

Henry Ford (American manufacturer)

MON
[date]

today's goal

route | distance |
notes | time |
    workout |
    heart rate |
    morning hr |
    weather |
    x training |

TUE
[date]

today's goal

route | distance |
notes | time |
    workout |
    heart rate |
    morning hr |
    weather |
    x training |

WED
[date]

today's goal

route | distance |
notes | time |
    workout |
    heart rate |
    morning hr |
    weather |
    x training |

THU
[date]

today's goal

route | distance |
notes | time |
    workout |
    heart rate |
    morning hr |
    weather |
    x training |

Week 20

FRI
[date]
today's goal

route
notes

distance
time
workout
heart rate
morning hr
weather
x training

SAT
[date]
today's goal

route
notes

distance
time
workout
heart rate
morning hr
weather
x training

SUN
[date]
today's goal

route
notes

distance
time
workout
heart rate
morning hr
weather
x training

NOTES

Distance for week
Time for week
Distance to date
End of week weight
Total mileage on shoes
End of week hr

Anyone can win, unless there happens to be a second entry.

George Ade

MON

[date]

today's goal

route | distance |
notes | time |
workout |
heart rate |
morning hr |
weather |
x training |

TUE

[date]

today's goal

route | distance |
notes | time |
workout |
heart rate |
morning hr |
weather |
x training |

WED

[date]

today's goal

route | distance |
notes | time |
workout |
heart rate |
morning hr |
weather |
x training |

THU

[date]

today's goal

route | distance |
notes | time |
workout |
heart rate |
morning hr |
weather |
x training |

Week 21

FRI
[date]

today's goal

route |
notes |

distance |
time |
workout |
heart rate |
morning hr |
weather |
x training |

SAT
[date]

today's goal

route |
notes |

distance |
time |
workout |
heart rate |
morning hr |
weather |
x training |

SUN
[date]

today's goal

route |
notes |

distance |
time |
workout |
heart rate |
morning hr |
weather |
x training |

NOTES

Distance for week
Time for week
Distance to date
End of week weight
Total mileage on shoes
End of week hr

Suffering is the sole origin of consciousness.

Dostoyevsky (Russian writer)

MON
[date]

today's goal

route | distance |
notes | time |
| workout |
| heart rate |
| morning hr |
| weather |
| x training |

TUE
[date]

today's goal

route | distance |
notes | time |
| workout |
| heart rate |
| morning hr |
| weather |
| x training |

WED
[date]

today's goal

route | distance |
notes | time |
| workout |
| heart rate |
| morning hr |
| weather |
| x training |

THU
[date]

today's goal

route | distance |
notes | time |
| workout |
| heart rate |
| morning hr |
| weather |
| x training |

Week 22

FRI
[date]

today's goal

route |
notes |

distance |
time |
workout |
heart rate |
morning hr |
weather |
x training |

SAT
[date]

today's goal

route |
notes |

distance |
time |
workout |
heart rate |
morning hr |
weather |
x training |

SUN
[date]

today's goal

route |
notes |

distance |
time |
workout |
heart rate |
morning hr |
weather |
x training |

NOTES

Distance for week
Time for week
Distance to date
End of week weight
Total mileage on shoes
End of week hr

When was the last time you did something for the first time?

Sally Edwards (athlete, author, motivator)

MON
[date]

today's goal

route | distance |
notes | time |
workout |
heart rate |
morning hr |
weather |
x training |

TUE
[date]

today's goal

route | distance |
notes | time |
workout |
heart rate |
morning hr |
weather |
x training |

WED
[date]

today's goal

route | distance |
notes | time |
workout |
heart rate |
morning hr |
weather |
x training |

THU
[date]

today's goal

route | distance |
notes | time |
workout |
heart rate |
morning hr |
weather |
x training |

Week 23

FRI

[date]

today's goal

route |
notes |

distance |
time |
workout |
heart rate |
morning hr |
weather |
x training |

SAT

[date]

today's goal

route |
notes |

distance |
time |
workout |
heart rate |
morning hr |
weather |
x training |

SUN

[date]

today's goal

route |
notes |

distance |
time |
workout |
heart rate |
morning hr |
weather |
x training |

NOTES

Distance for week
Time for week
Distance to date
End of week weight
Total mileage on shoes
End of week hr

Long slow distance makes long slow runners.

Jim Bush (American track coach)

MON
[date]

today's goal

route |
notes |

distance |
time |
workout |
heart rate |
morning hr |
weather |
x training |

TUE
[date]

today's goal

route |
notes |

distance |
time |
workout |
heart rate |
morning hr |
weather |
x training |

WED
[date]

today's goal

route |
notes |

distance |
time |
workout |
heart rate |
morning hr |
weather |
x training |

THU
[date]

today's goal

route |
notes |

distance |
time |
workout |
heart rate |
morning hr |
weather |
x training |

FRI [date]

today's goal

route |
notes |

distance |
time |
workout |
heart rate |
morning hr |
weather |
x training |

SAT [date]

today's goal

route |
notes |

distance |
time |
workout |
heart rate |
morning hr |
weather |
x training |

SUN [date]

today's goal

route |
notes |

distance |
time |
workout |
heart rate |
morning hr |
weather |
x training |

NOTES

Distance for week
Time for week
Distance to date
End of week weight
Total mileage on shoes
End of week hr

All I know is that people don't throw beer cans at me when I run anymore.

John J. Kelley (Boston Marathon champion)

MON
[date]

today's goal

route |
notes |

distance |
time |
workout |
heart rate |
morning hr |
weather |
x training |

TUE
[date]

today's goal

route |
notes |

distance |
time |
workout |
heart rate |
morning hr |
weather |
x training |

WED
[date]

today's goal

route |
notes |

distance |
time |
workout |
heart rate |
morning hr |
weather |
x training |

THU
[date]

today's goal

route |
notes |

distance |
time |
workout |
heart rate |
morning hr |
weather |
x training |

Week 25

FRI
[date]

today's goal

route
notes

distance
time
workout
heart rate
morning hr
weather
x training

SAT
[date]

today's goal

route
notes

distance
time
workout
heart rate
morning hr
weather
x training

SUN
[date]

today's goal

route
notes

distance
time
workout
heart rate
morning hr
weather
x training

NOTES

Distance for week
Time for week
Distance to date
End of week weight
Total mileage on shoes
End of week hr

Hills are speedwork in disguise.

Frank Shorter (American Olympic champion)

MON
[date]

| route | | distance | |
| notes | | time | |

today's goal
- workout
- heart rate
- morning hr
- weather
- x training

TUE
[date]

| route | | distance | |
| notes | | time | |

today's goal
- workout
- heart rate
- morning hr
- weather
- x training

WED
[date]

| route | | distance | |
| notes | | time | |

today's goal
- workout
- heart rate
- morning hr
- weather
- x training

THU
[date]

| route | | distance | |
| notes | | time | |

today's goal
- workout
- heart rate
- morning hr
- weather
- x training

Week 26

FRI [date]

today's goal

route |
notes |

distance |
time |
workout |
heart rate |
morning hr |
weather |
x training |

SAT [date]

today's goal

route |
notes |

distance |
time |
workout |
heart rate |
morning hr |
weather |
x training |

SUN [date]

today's goal

route |
notes |

distance |
time |
workout |
heart rate |
morning hr |
weather |
x training |

NOTES

Distance for week
Time for week
Distance to date
End of week weight
Total mileage on shoes
End of week hr

The only limits are, as usual, those of vision.

James Broughton (American poet)

MON

[date]

today's goal

route |
notes |

distance |
time |
workout |
heart rate |
morning hr |
weather |
x training |

TUE

[date]

today's goal

route |
notes |

distance |
time |
workout |
heart rate |
morning hr |
weather |
x training |

WED

[date]

today's goal

route |
notes |

distance |
time |
workout |
heart rate |
morning hr |
weather |
x training |

THU

[date]

today's goal

route |
notes |

distance |
time |
workout |
heart rate |
morning hr |
weather |
x training |

Week 27

FRI

[date]

today's goal

route |
notes |

distance |
time |
workout |
heart rate |
morning hr |
weather |
x training |

SAT

[date]

today's goal

route |
notes |

distance |
time |
workout |
heart rate |
morning hr |
weather |
x training |

SUN

[date]

today's goal

route |
notes |

distance |
time |
workout |
heart rate |
morning hr |
weather |
x training |

NOTES

Distance for week
Time for week
Distance to date
End of week weight
Total mileage on shoes
End of week hr

A lot of people run to see who's the fastest. I run to see who has the most guts.

Steve Prefontaine (American Olympian)

MON
[date]

today's goal

route | distance |
notes | time |

workout |

heart rate |

morning hr |

weather |

x training |

TUE
[date]

today's goal

route |

notes |

distance |

time |

workout |

heart rate |

morning hr |

weather |

x training |

WED
[date]

today's goal

route |

notes |

distance |

time |

workout |

heart rate |

morning hr |

weather |

x training |

THU
[date]

today's goal

route |

notes |

distance |

time |

workout |

heart rate |

morning hr |

weather |

x training |

Week ___ 28

FRI
[date]

today's goal

route |
notes |

distance |
time |
workout |
heart rate |
morning hr |
weather |
x training |

SAT
[date]

today's goal

route |
notes |

distance |
time |
workout |
heart rate |
morning hr |
weather |
x training |

SUN
[date]

today's goal

route |
notes |

distance |
time |
workout |
heart rate |
morning hr |
weather |
x training |

NOTES

Distance for week
Time for week
Distance to date
End of week weight
Total mileage on shoes
End of week hr

The difference between a jogger and a runner is an entry blank.

Dr. George Sheehan (American runner & writer)

MON
[date]

today's goal

route |
notes |

distance |
time |
workout |
heart rate |
morning hr |
weather |
x training |

TUE
[date]

today's goal

route |
notes |

distance |
time |
workout |
heart rate |
morning hr |
weather |
x training |

WED
[date]

today's goal

route |
notes |

distance |
time |
workout |
heart rate |
morning hr |
weather |
x training |

THU
[date]

today's goal

route |
notes |

distance |
time |
workout |
heart rate |
morning hr |
weather |
x training |

Week 29

FRI
[date]

today's goal

route |
notes |

distance |
time |
workout |
heart rate |
morning hr |
weather |
x training |

SAT
[date]

today's goal

route |
notes |

distance |
time |
workout |
heart rate |
morning hr |
weather |
x training |

SUN
[date]

today's goal

route |
notes |

distance |
time |
workout |
heart rate |
morning hr |
weather |
x training |

NOTES

Distance for week
Time for week
Distance to date
End of week weight
Total mileage on shoes
End of week hr

...Life, by definition, is never still.

Kurt Vonnegut, Jr. (American writer)

MON
[date]

today's goal

route
notes

distance
time
workout
heart rate
morning hr
weather
x training

TUE
[date]

today's goal

route
notes

distance
time
workout
heart rate
morning hr
weather
x training

WED
[date]

today's goal

route
notes

distance
time
workout
heart rate
morning hr
weather
x training

THU
[date]

today's goal

route
notes

distance
time
workout
heart rate
morning hr
weather
x training

Week ___ 30

FRI
[date]

today's goal

route |
notes |

distance |
time |
workout |
heart rate |
morning hr |
weather |
x training |

SAT
[date]

today's goal

route |
notes |

distance |
time |
workout |
heart rate |
morning hr |
weather |
x training |

SUN
[date]

today's goal

route |
notes |

distance |
time |
workout |
heart rate |
morning hr |
weather |
x training |

NOTES

Distance for week
Time for week
Distance to date
End of week weight
Total mileage on shoes
End of week hr

You might be a runner if you wear out shoes faster than your five-year old.

Tim Martin (American runner & writer)

MON
[date]

today's goal

route		distance	
notes		time	
		workout	
		heart rate	
		morning hr	
		weather	
		x training	

TUE
[date]

today's goal

route		distance	
notes		time	
		workout	
		heart rate	
		morning hr	
		weather	
		x training	

WED
[date]

today's goal

route		distance	
notes		time	
		workout	
		heart rate	
		morning hr	
		weather	
		x training	

THU
[date]

today's goal

route		distance	
notes		time	
		workout	
		heart rate	
		morning hr	
		weather	
		x training	

Week 31

FRI
[date]

today's goal

route
notes

distance
time
workout
heart rate
morning hr
weather
x training

SAT
[date]

today's goal

route
notes

distance
time
workout
heart rate
morning hr
weather
x training

SUN
[date]

today's goal

route
notes

distance
time
workout
heart rate
morning hr
weather
x training

NOTES

Distance for week
Time for week
Distance to date
End of week weight
Total mileage on shoes
End of week hr

Life doesn't run away from nobody. Life runs at people.

Joe Frazier (American boxer)

MON

[date]

today's goal

route		distance	
notes		time	
		workout	
		heart rate	
		morning hr	
		weather	
		x training	

TUE

[date]

today's goal

route		distance	
notes		time	
		workout	
		heart rate	
		morning hr	
		weather	
		x training	

WED

[date]

today's goal

route		distance	
notes		time	
		workout	
		heart rate	
		morning hr	
		weather	
		x training	

THU

[date]

today's goal

route		distance	
notes		time	
		workout	
		heart rate	
		morning hr	
		weather	
		x training	

Week 32

FRI
[date]

today's goal

route
notes

distance
time
workout
heart rate
morning hr
weather
x training

SAT
[date]

today's goal

route
notes

distance
time
workout
heart rate
morning hr
weather
x training

SUN
[date]

today's goal

route
notes

distance
time
workout
heart rate
morning hr
weather
x training

NOTES

Distance for week
Time for week
Distance to date
End of week weight
Total mileage on shoes
End of week hr

I love running cross country....On a track, I feel like a hamster.

Robin Williams (American actor & comedian)

MON

[date]

today's goal

route |
notes |

distance |
time |
workout |
heart rate |
morning hr |
weather |
x training |

TUE

[date]

today's goal

route |
notes |

distance |
time |
workout |
heart rate |
morning hr |
weather |
x training |

WED

[date]

today's goal

route |
notes |

distance |
time |
workout |
heart rate |
morning hr |
weather |
x training |

THU

[date]

today's goal

route |
notes |

distance |
time |
workout |
heart rate |
morning hr |
weather |
x training |

Week ___ 33 ___

FRI
[date]
today's goal

route |
notes |

distance |
time |
workout |
heart rate |
morning hr |
weather |
x training |

SAT
[date]
today's goal

route |
notes |

distance |
time |
workout |
heart rate |
morning hr |
weather |
x training |

SUN
[date]
today's goal

route |
notes |

distance |
time |
workout |
heart rate |
morning hr |
weather |
x training |

NOTES

Distance for week
Time for week
Distance to date
End of week weight
Total mileage on shoes
End of week hr

Our bodies are our gardens — our wills are our gardeners.

William Shakespeare

MON
[date]

today's goal

route | distance |
notes | time |
    workout |
    heart rate |
    morning hr |
    weather |
    x training |

TUE
[date]

today's goal

route | distance |
notes | time |
    workout |
    heart rate |
    morning hr |
    weather |
    x training |

WED
[date]

today's goal

route | distance |
notes | time |
    workout |
    heart rate |
    morning hr |
    weather |
    x training |

THU
[date]

today's goal

route | distance |
notes | time |
    workout |
    heart rate |
    morning hr |
    weather |
    x training |

Week 34 [week of:]

FRI
[date]

today's goal

route	distance
notes	time
	workout
	heart rate
	morning hr
	weather
	x training

SAT
[date]

today's goal

route	distance
notes	time
	workout
	heart rate
	morning hr
	weather
	x training

SUN
[date]

today's goal

route	distance
notes	time
	workout
	heart rate
	morning hr
	weather
	x training

NOTES

Distance for week

Time for week

Distance to date

End of week weight

Total mileage on shoes

End of week hr

If there is no struggle, there is no progress.

Frederick Douglass (American writer & abolitionist)

MON

[date]

route

notes

today's goal

distance

time

workout

heart rate

morning hr

weather

x training

TUE

[date]

route

notes

today's goal

distance

time

workout

heart rate

morning hr

weather

x training

WED

[date]

route

notes

today's goal

distance

time

workout

heart rate

morning hr

weather

x training

THU

[date]

route

notes

today's goal

distance

time

workout

heart rate

morning hr

weather

x training

Week — 35

[week of:]

FRI
[date]

today's goal

route |
notes |

distance |
time |
workout |
heart rate |
morning hr |
weather |
x training |

SAT
[date]

today's goal

route |
notes |

distance |
time |
workout |
heart rate |
morning hr |
weather |
x training |

SUN
[date]

today's goal

route |
notes |

distance |
time |
workout |
heart rate |
morning hr |
weather |
x training |

NOTES

Distance for week
Time for week
Distance to date
End of week weight
Total mileage on shoes
End of week hr

If the hill has its own name, then it's probably a pretty tough hill.

Marty Stern (American track coach)

MON [date]

today's goal

route		distance	
notes		time	
		workout	
		heart rate	
		morning hr	
		weather	
		x training	

TUE [date]

today's goal

route		distance	
notes		time	
		workout	
		heart rate	
		morning hr	
		weather	
		x training	

WED [date]

today's goal

route		distance	
notes		time	
		workout	
		heart rate	
		morning hr	
		weather	
		x training	

THU [date]

today's goal

route		distance	
notes		time	
		workout	
		heart rate	
		morning hr	
		weather	
		x training	

FRI

[date]

today's goal

route

notes

distance

time

workout

heart rate

morning hr

weather

x training

SAT

[date]

today's goal

route

notes

distance

time

workout

heart rate

morning hr

weather

x training

SUN

[date]

today's goal

route

notes

distance

time

workout

heart rate

morning hr

weather

x training

NOTES

Distance for week

Time for week

Distance to date

End of week weight

Total mileage on shoes

End of week hr

Walking isn't a lost art—one must, by some means, get to the garage.

Evan Esar

MON
[date]

today's goal

route |
notes |

distance |
time |
workout |
heart rate |
morning hr |
weather |
x training |

TUE
[date]

today's goal

route |
notes |

distance |
time |
workout |
heart rate |
morning hr |
weather |
x training |

WED
[date]

today's goal

route |
notes |

distance |
time |
workout |
heart rate |
morning hr |
weather |
x training |

THU
[date]

today's goal

route |
notes |

distance |
time |
workout |
heart rate |
morning hr |
weather |
x training |

[week of:]

FRI
[date]

route |
notes |

today's goal

distance |
time |
workout |
heart rate |
morning hr |
weather |
x training |

SAT
[date]

route |
notes |

today's goal

distance |
time |
workout |
heart rate |
morning hr |
weather |
x training |

SUN
[date]

route |
notes |

today's goal

distance |
time |
workout |
heart rate |
morning hr |
weather |
x training |

NOTES ·

Distance for week
Time for week
Distance to date
End of week weight
Total mileage on shoes
End of week hr

I don't train. I just run my 3-15 miles a day.

Jack Foster (New Zealand Olympian)

MON
[date]

today's goal

route | distance |
notes | time |
    workout |
    heart rate |
    morning hr |
    weather |
    x training |

TUE
[date]

today's goal

route | distance |
notes | time |
    workout |
    heart rate |
    morning hr |
    weather |
    x training |

WED
[date]

today's goal

route | distance |
notes | time |
    workout |
    heart rate |
    morning hr |
    weather |
    x training |

THU
[date]

today's goal

route | distance |
notes | time |
    workout |
    heart rate |
    morning hr |
    weather |
    x training |

Week 38

FRI

[date]

today's goal

route |
notes |

distance |
time |
workout |
heart rate |
morning hr |
weather |
x training |

SAT

[date]

today's goal

route |
notes |

distance |
time |
workout |
heart rate |
morning hr |
weather |
x training |

SUN

[date]

today's goal

route |
notes |

distance |
time |
workout |
heart rate |
morning hr |
weather |
x training |

NOTES

Distance for week
Time for week
Distance to date
End of week weight
Total mileage on shoes
End of week hr

You cannot propel yourself forward by patting yourself on the back.

Anonymous

MON

[date]

today's goal

route	distance
notes	time
	workout
	heart rate
	morning hr
	weather
	x training

TUE

[date]

today's goal

route	distance
notes	time
	workout
	heart rate
	morning hr
	weather
	x training

WED

[date]

today's goal

route	distance
notes	time
	workout
	heart rate
	morning hr
	weather
	x training

THU

[date]

today's goal

route	distance
notes	time
	workout
	heart rate
	morning hr
	weather
	x training

Week 39

FRI
[date]

today's goal

route
notes

distance
time
workout
heart rate
morning hr
weather
x training

SAT
[date]

today's goal

route
notes

distance
time
workout
heart rate
morning hr
weather
x training

SUN
[date]

today's goal

route
notes

distance
time
workout
heart rate
morning hr
weather
x training

NOTES

Distance for week
Time for week
Distance to date
End of week weight
Total mileage on shoes
End of week hr

The price of excellence is discipline. The cost of mediocrity is disappointment.

William W. Ward

MON
[date]

route |
notes |

today's goal

distance |
time |
workout |
heart rate |
morning hr |
weather |
x training |

TUE
[date]

route |
notes |

today's goal

distance |
time |
workout |
heart rate |
morning hr |
weather |
x training |

WED
[date]

route |
notes |

today's goal

distance |
time |
workout |
heart rate |
morning hr |
weather |
x training |

THU
[date]

route |
notes |

today's goal

distance |
time |
workout |
heart rate |
morning hr |
weather |
x training |

Week __ 40

FRI

[date]

| route | | distance |
| notes | | time |

today's goal

workout

heart rate

morning hr

weather

x training

SAT

[date]

| route | | distance |
| notes | | time |

today's goal

workout

heart rate

morning hr

weather

x training

SUN

[date]

| route | | distance |
| notes | | time |

today's goal

workout

heart rate

morning hr

weather

x training

NOTES

Distance for week

Time for week

Distance to date

End of week weight

Total mileage on shoes

End of week hr

...When I see someone running on my street, my instincts tell me to let the dog out after him.

Mike Royko (American newspaper columnist)

MON
[date]

route | distance |
notes | time |
today's goal | workout |
| heart rate |
| morning hr |
| weather |
| x training |

TUE
[date]

route | distance |
notes | time |
today's goal | workout |
| heart rate |
| morning hr |
| weather |
| x training |

WED
[date]

route | distance |
notes | time |
today's goal | workout |
| heart rate |
| morning hr |
| weather |
| x training |

THU
[date]

route | distance |
notes | time |
today's goal | workout |
| heart rate |
| morning hr |
| weather |
| x training |

Week 41

FRI
[date]

today's goal

route
notes

distance
time
workout
heart rate
morning hr
weather
x training

SAT
[date]

today's goal

route
notes

distance
time
workout
heart rate
morning hr
weather
x training

SUN
[date]

today's goal

route
notes

distance
time
workout
heart rate
morning hr
weather
x training

NOTES

Distance for week
Time for week
Distance to date
End of week weight
Total mileage on shoes
End of week hr

You entered a marathon with hills? You idiot.

Don Kardong (American writer & Olympian)

MON

[date]

today's goal

route		distance	
notes		time	
		workout	
		heart rate	
		morning hr	
		weather	
		x training	

TUE

[date]

today's goal

route		distance	
notes		time	
		workout	
		heart rate	
		morning hr	
		weather	
		x training	

WED

[date]

today's goal

route		distance	
notes		time	
		workout	
		heart rate	
		morning hr	
		weather	
		x training	

THU

[date]

today's goal

route		distance	
notes		time	
		workout	
		heart rate	
		morning hr	
		weather	
		x training	

Week 42

FRI

[date]

today's goal

route |
notes |

distance |
time |
workout |
heart rate |
morning hr |
weather |
x training |

SAT

[date]

today's goal

route |
notes |

distance |
time |
workout |
heart rate |
morning hr |
weather |
x training |

SUN

[date]

today's goal

route |
notes |

distance |
time |
workout |
heart rate |
morning hr |
weather |
x training |

NOTES

Distance for week
Time for week
Distance to date
End of week weight
Total mileage on shoes
End of week hr

No one ever won the olive wreath with an impressive training diary.

Marty Liquori (American Olympian)

MON
[date]

today's goal

route
notes

distance
time
workout
heart rate
morning hr
weather
x training

TUE
[date]

today's goal

route
notes

distance
time
workout
heart rate
morning hr
weather
x training

WED
[date]

today's goal

route
notes

distance
time
workout
heart rate
morning hr
weather
x training

THU
[date]

today's goal

route
notes

distance
time
workout
heart rate
morning hr
weather
x training

Week 43

FRI
[date]

today's goal

route
notes

distance
time
workout
heart rate
morning hr
weather
x training

SAT
[date]

today's goal

route
notes

distance
time
workout
heart rate
morning hr
weather
x training

SUN
[date]

today's goal

route
notes

distance
time
workout
heart rate
morning hr
weather
x training

NOTES

Distance for week
Time for week
Distance to date
End of week weight
Total mileage on shoes
End of week hr

I'm not going to stand at the start...on the Verrazano Narrows Bridge and get peed on.

Radio host Don Imus on why he won't run the NYC Marathon

MON
[date]

route | distance |
notes | time |

today's goal

workout |
heart rate |
morning hr |
weather |
x training |

TUE
[date]

route | distance |
notes | time |

today's goal

workout |
heart rate |
morning hr |
weather |
x training |

WED
[date]

route | distance |
notes | time |

today's goal

workout |
heart rate |
morning hr |
weather |
x training |

THU
[date]

route | distance |
notes | time |

today's goal

workout |
heart rate |
morning hr |
weather |
x training |

Week 44

FRI

[date]

today's goal

route |
notes |

distance |
time |
workout |
heart rate |
morning hr |
weather |
x training |

SAT

[date]

today's goal

route |
notes |

distance |
time |
workout |
heart rate |
morning hr |
weather |
x training |

SUN

[date]

today's goal

route |
notes |

distance |
time |
workout |
heart rate |
morning hr |
weather |
x training |

NOTES

Distance for week
Time for week
Distance to date
End of week weight
Total mileage on shoes
End of week hr

Bid me run, and I will strive for things impossible.

William Shakespeare (English writer & poet)

MON
[date]

route | distance |

notes | time |

today's goal

workout |

heart rate |

morning hr |

weather |

x training |

TUE
[date]

route | distance |

notes | time |

today's goal

workout |

heart rate |

morning hr |

weather |

x training |

WED
[date]

route | distance |

notes | time |

today's goal

workout |

heart rate |

morning hr |

weather |

x training |

THU
[date]

route | distance |

notes | time |

today's goal

workout |

heart rate |

morning hr |

weather |

x training |

Week 45

FRI   [date]

route

notes

today's goal

distance

time

workout

heart rate

morning hr

weather

x training

SAT   [date]

route

notes

today's goal

distance

time

workout

heart rate

morning hr

weather

x training

SUN   [date]

route

notes

today's goal

distance

time

workout

heart rate

morning hr

weather

x training

NOTES

Distance for week

Time for week

Distance to date

End of week weight

Total mileage on shoes

End of week hr

The only easy day was yesterday.

USN seal HQ motto

MON
[date]

today's goal

route | distance |
notes | time |
       workout |
       heart rate |
       morning hr |
       weather |
       x training |

TUE
[date]

today's goal

route | distance |
notes | time |
       workout |
       heart rate |
       morning hr |
       weather |
       x training |

WED
[date]

today's goal

route | distance |
notes | time |
       workout |
       heart rate |
       morning hr |
       weather |
       x training |

THU
[date]

today's goal

route | distance |
notes | time |
       workout |
       heart rate |
       morning hr |
       weather |
       x training |

Week 46

FRI

[date]

today's goal

route |
notes |

distance |
time |
workout |
heart rate |
morning hr |
weather |
x training |

SAT

[date]

today's goal

route |
notes |

distance |
time |
workout |
heart rate |
morning hr |
weather |
x training |

SUN

[date]

today's goal

route |
notes |

distance |
time |
workout |
heart rate |
morning hr |
weather |
x training |

NOTES

Distance for week
Time for week
Distance to date
End of week weight
Total mileage on shoes
End of week hr

I now have only good days, or great days.

Lance Armstrong

MON

[date]

today's goal

route |
notes |

distance |
time |
workout |
heart rate |
morning hr |
weather |
x training |

TUE

[date]

today's goal

route |
notes |

distance |
time |
workout |
heart rate |
morning hr |
weather |
x training |

WED

[date]

today's goal

route |
notes |

distance |
time |
workout |
heart rate |
morning hr |
weather |
x training |

THU

[date]

today's goal

route |
notes |

distance |
time |
workout |
heart rate |
morning hr |
weather |
x training |

Week 47

FRI [date]

route |
notes |

today's goal

distance |
time |
workout |
heart rate |
morning hr |
weather |
x training |

SAT [date]

route |
notes |

today's goal

distance |
time |
workout |
heart rate |
morning hr |
weather |
x training |

SUN [date]

route |
notes |

today's goal

distance |
time |
workout |
heart rate |
morning hr |
weather |
x training |

NOTES

Distance for week
Time for week
Distance to date
End of week weight
Total mileage on shoes
End of week hr

Long-distance running is particularly good training in perseverance.

Mao Tse-tung (Chinese Communist leader)

MON

[date]

today's goal

route |
notes |

distance |
time |
workout |
heart rate |
morning hr |
weather |
x training |

TUE

[date]

today's goal

route |
notes |

distance |
time |
workout |
heart rate |
morning hr |
weather |
x training |

WED

[date]

today's goal

route |
notes |

distance |
time |
workout |
heart rate |
morning hr |
weather |
x training |

THU

[date]

today's goal

route |
notes |

distance |
time |
workout |
heart rate |
morning hr |
weather |
x training |

Week 48

FRI

[date]

today's goal

route

notes

distance

time

workout

heart rate

morning hr

weather

x training

SAT

[date]

today's goal

route

notes

distance

time

workout

heart rate

morning hr

weather

x training

SUN

[date]

today's goal

route

notes

distance

time

workout

heart rate

morning hr

weather

x training

NOTES

Distance for week

Time for week

Distance to date

End of week weight

Total mileage on shoes

End of week hr

You have to forget your last marathon before you try another.

Frank Shorter (American Olympic champion)

MON
[date]

today's goal

route |
notes |

distance |
time |
workout |
heart rate |
morning hr |
weather |
x training |

TUE
[date]

today's goal

route |
notes |

distance |
time |
workout |
heart rate |
morning hr |
weather |
x training |

WED
[date]

today's goal

route |
notes |

distance |
time |
workout |
heart rate |
morning hr |
weather |
x training |

THU
[date]

today's goal

route |
notes |

distance |
time |
workout |
heart rate |
morning hr |
weather |
x training |

Week 49

FRI
[date]

today's goal

route
notes

distance
time
workout
heart rate
morning hr
weather
x training

SAT
[date]

today's goal

route
notes

distance
time
workout
heart rate
morning hr
weather
x training

SUN
[date]

today's goal

route
notes

distance
time
workout
heart rate
morning hr
weather
x training

NOTES

Distance for week
Time for week
Distance to date
End of week weight
Total mileage on shoes
End of week hr

Mental will is a muscle that needs exercise, just like muscles of the body.

Lynn Jennings (American Olympian)

MON

[date]

today's goal

route | distance |
notes | time |
workout |
heart rate |
morning hr |
weather |
x training |

TUE

[date]

today's goal

route | distance |
notes | time |
workout |
heart rate |
morning hr |
weather |
x training |

WED

[date]

today's goal

route | distance |
notes | time |
workout |
heart rate |
morning hr |
weather |
x training |

THU

[date]

today's goal

route | distance |
notes | time |
workout |
heart rate |
morning hr |
weather |
x training |

Week 50

FRI
[date]

today's goal

route |
notes |

distance |
time |
workout |
heart rate |
morning hr |
weather |
x training |

SAT
[date]

today's goal

route |
notes |

distance |
time |
workout |
heart rate |
morning hr |
weather |
x training |

SUN
[date]

today's goal

route |
notes |

distance |
time |
workout |
heart rate |
morning hr |
weather |
x training |

NOTES

Distance for week
Time for week
Distance to date
End of week weight
Total mileage on shoes
End of week hr

Run slowly, run daily, drink moderately and don't eat like a pig.

Dr. Ernest van Aaken (German coach)

MON
[date]

route		distance	
notes		time	
today's goal		workout	
		heart rate	
		morning hr	
		weather	
		x training	

TUE
[date]

route		distance	
notes		time	
today's goal		workout	
		heart rate	
		morning hr	
		weather	
		x training	

WED
[date]

route		distance	
notes		time	
today's goal		workout	
		heart rate	
		morning hr	
		weather	
		x training	

THU
[date]

route		distance	
notes		time	
today's goal		workout	
		heart rate	
		morning hr	
		weather	
		x training	

Week 51

FRI

[date]

route

notes

today's goal

distance

time

workout

heart rate

morning hr

weather

x training

SAT

[date]

route

notes

today's goal

distance

time

workout

heart rate

morning hr

weather

x training

SUN

[date]

route

notes

today's goal

distance

time

workout

heart rate

morning hr

weather

x training

NOTES

Distance for week

Time for week

Distance to date

End of week weight

Total mileage on shoes

End of week hr

Some might say that it's easier to be the runner than the runner's family.

Rob de Castella (Australian marathon champion)

MON
[date]

| route | distance |
| notes | time |

today's goal

workout
heart rate
morning hr
weather
x training

TUE
[date]

| route | distance |
| notes | time |

today's goal

workout
heart rate
morning hr
weather
x training

WED
[date]

| route | distance |
| notes | time |

today's goal

workout
heart rate
morning hr
weather
x training

THU
[date]

| route | distance |
| notes | time |

today's goal

workout
heart rate
morning hr
weather
x training

Week 52

[week of:]

FRI

[date]

today's goal

route	
notes	

distance	
time	
workout	
heart rate	
morning hr	
weather	
x training	

SAT

[date]

today's goal

route	
notes	

distance	
time	
workout	
heart rate	
morning hr	
weather	
x training	

SUN

[date]

today's goal

route	
notes	

distance	
time	
workout	
heart rate	
morning hr	
weather	
x training	

NOTES

Distance for week	
Time for week	
Distance to date	
End of week weight	
Total mileage on shoes	
End of week hr	

One chance is all you need.

Jesse Owens (American 4-Time Olympic gold medalist)

MON
[date]

today's goal

route |
notes |

distance |
time |
workout |
heart rate |
morning hr |
weather |
x training |

TUE
[date]

today's goal

route |
notes |

distance |
time |
workout |
heart rate |
morning hr |
weather |
x training |

WED
[date]

today's goal

route |
notes |

distance |
time |
workout |
heart rate |
morning hr |
weather |
x training |

THU
[date]

today's goal

route |
notes |

distance |
time |
workout |
heart rate |
morning hr |
weather |
x training |

Week ___ 53

FRI
[date]

route
notes

today's goal

distance
time
workout
heart rate
morning hr
weather
x training

SAT
[date]

route
notes

today's goal

distance
time
workout
heart rate
morning hr
weather
x training

SUN
[date]

route
notes

today's goal

distance
time
workout
heart rate
morning hr
weather
x training

NOTES

Distance for week
Time for week
Distance to date
End of week weight
Total mileage on shoes
End of week hr

GOAL MAP

Week 1 Goal

Date	Goal	Actual
M		
T		
W		
Th		
F		
S		
S		

Totals _____ _____

Comments _____

Week 2 Goal _____

Date	Goal	Actual
M		
T		
W		
Th		
F		
S		
S		

Totals _____ _____

Comments _____

Week 3 Goal

Date	Goal	Actual
M		
T		
W		
Th		
F		
S		
S		

Totals _____ _____

Comments _____

Week 4 Goal

Date	Goal	Actual
M		
T		
W		
Th		
F		
S		
S		

Totals _____ _____

Comments _____

Week 5 Goal

Date	Goal	Actual
M		
T		
W		
Th		
F		
S		
S		
Totals		

Comments _____

Week 7 Goal

Date	Goal	Actual
M		
T		
W		
Th		
F		
S		
S		
Totals		

Comments _____

Week 6 Goal

Date	Goal	Actual
M		
T		
W		
Th		
F		
S		
S		
Totals		

Comments _____

Week 8 Goal _____

Date	Goal	Actual
M		
T		
W		
Th		
F		
S		
S		
Totals		

Comments _____

GOAL MAP

Week 9 Goal

Date	Goal	Actual
M		
T		
W		
Th		
F		
S		
S		
Totals		
Comments		

Week 11 Goal

Date	Goal	Actual
M		
T		
W		
Th		
F		
S		
S		
Totals		
Comments		

Week 10 Goal _____

Date	Goal	Actual
M		
T		
W		
Th		
F		
S		
S		
Totals		
Comments		

Week 12 Goal

Date	Goal	Actual
M		
T		
W		
Th		
F		
S		
S		
Totals		
Comments		

GOAL

Week 13 Goal

Date	Goal	Actual
M		
T		
W		
Th		
F		
S		
S		
Totals		
Comments		

Week 14 Goal

Date	Goal	Actual
M		
T		
W		
Th		
F		
S		
S		
Totals		
Comments		

Week 15 Goal

Date	Goal	Actual
M		
T		
W		
Th		
F		
S		
S		
Totals		
Comments		

Week 16 Goal _____

Date	Goal	Actual
M		
T		
W		
Th		
F		
S		
S		
Totals		
Comments		

Week 17 Goal

Date	Goal	Actual
M		
T		
W		
Th		
F		
S		
S		
Totals		

Comments _____

Week 19 Goal

Date	Goal	Actual
M		
T		
W		
Th		
F		
S		
S		
Totals		

Comments _____

Week 18 Goal _____

Date	Goal	Actual
M		
T		
W		
Th		
F		
S		
S		
Totals		

Comments _____

Week 20 Goal

Date	Goal	Actual
M		
T		
W		
Th		
F		
S		
S		
Totals		

Comments _____

Week 21 Goal

Date	Goal	Actual
M		
T		
W		
Th		
F		
S		
S		
Totals		
Comments		

Week 23 Goal

Date	Goal	Actual
M		
T		
W		
Th		
F		
S		
S		
Totals		
Comments		

Week 22 Goal

Date	Goal	Actual
M		
T		
W		
Th		
F		
S		
S		
Totals		
Comments		

Week 24 Goal _____

Date	Goal	Actual
M		
T		
W		
Th		
F		
S		
S		
Totals		
Comments		

Week 25 Goal

Date	Goal	Actual
M		
T		
W		
Th		
F		
S		
S		
Totals		

Comments _____

Week 27 Goal

Date	Goal	Actual
M		
T		
W		
Th		
F		
S		
S		
Totals		

Comments _____

Week 26 Goal _____

Date	Goal	Actual
M		
T		
W		
Th		
F		
S		
S		
Totals		

Comments _____

Week 28 Goal

Date	Goal	Actual
M		
T		
W		
Th		
F		
S		
S		
Totals		

Comments _____

Week 29 Goal

Date	Goal	Actual
M		
T		
W		
Th		
F		
S		
S		

Totals

Comments

Week 30 Goal

Date	Goal	Actual
M		
T		
W		
Th		
F		
S		
S		

Totals

Comments

Week 31 Goal

Date	Goal	Actual
M		
T		
W		
Th		
F		
S		
S		

Totals

Comments

Week 32 Goal

Date	Goal	Actual
M		
T		
W		
Th		
F		
S		
S		

Totals

Comments

Week 33 Goal

Date	Goal	Actual
M		
T		
W		
Th		
F		
S		
S		
Totals		

Comments _____

Week 35 Goal

Date	Goal	Actual
M		
T		
W		
Th		
F		
S		
S		
Totals		

Comments _____

Week 34 Goal _____

Date	Goal	Actual
M		
T		
W		
Th		
F		
S		
S		
Totals		

Comments _____

Week 36 Goal

Date	Goal	Actual
M		
T		
W		
Th		
F		
S		
S		
Totals		

Comments _____

Week 37 Goal

Date	Goal	Actual
M		
T		
W		
Th		
F		
S		
S		
Totals		

Comments _____

Week 38 Goal

Date	Goal	Actual
M		
T		
W		
Th		
F		
S		
S		
Totals		

Comments _____

Week 39 Goal

Date	Goal	Actual
M		
T		
W		
Th		
F		
S		
S		
Totals		

Comments _____

Week 40 Goal _____

Date	Goal	Actual
M		
T		
W		
Th		
F		
S		
S		
Totals		

Comments _____

GOAL MAP

Week 41 Goal

Date	Goal	Actual
M		
T		
W		
Th		
F		
S		
S		
Totals		

Comments _____

Week 42 Goal _____

Date	Goal	Actual
M		
T		
W		
Th		
F		
S		
S		
Totals		

Comments _____

Week 43 Goal

Date	Goal	Actual
M		
T		
W		
Th		
F		
S		
S		
Totals		

Comments _____

Week 44 Goal

Date	Goal	Actual
M		
T		
W		
Th		
F		
S		
S		
Totals		

Comments _____

Week 45 Goal

Date	Goal	Actual
M		
T		
W		
Th		
F		
S		
S		
Totals		

Comments _____

Week 46 Goal

Date	Goal	Actual
M		
T		
W		
Th		
F		
S		
S		
Totals		

Comments _____

Week 47 Goal

Date	Goal	Actual
M		
T		
W		
Th		
F		
S		
S		
Totals		

Comments _____

Week 48 Goal _____

Date	Goal	Actual
M		
T		
W		
Th		
F		
S		
S		
Totals		

Comments _____

Week 49 Goal

Date	Goal	Actual
M		
T		
W		
Th		
F		
S		
S		
Totals		
Comments		

Week 50 Goal _____

Date	Goal	Actual
M		
T		
W		
Th		
F		
S		
S		
Totals		
Comments		

Week 51 Goal

Date	Goal	Actual
M		
T		
W		
Th		
F		
S		
S		
Totals		
Comments		

Week 52 Goal

Date	Goal	Actual
M		
T		
W		
Th		
F		
S		
S		
Totals		
Comments		

DATE	RACE	DISTANCE	TIME	COMMENTS

DATE	RACE	DISTANCE	TIME	COMMENTS

Course:

Date	Time	Comments

Course:

Date	Time	Comments

Course:

Date	Time	Comments

Course:

Date	Time	Comments

"Okay Clem, one kiss... but keep your tongue in this time!"

PART III   The Charts

Mile Pace	5K	8K	5M	10K	15K	10M	13.1M	30K	26.2M	50K	50M	100K	100M
4:50	15:01	24:02	24:10	30:02	45:03	48:20	1:03:22	1:30:06	2:06:43	2:30:10	4:01:40	5:00:21	8:03:20
5:00	15:32	24:51	25:00	31:04	46:36	50:00	1:05:33	1:33:13	2:11:06	2:35:21	4:10:00	5:10:42	8:20:00
5:10	16:03	25:41	25:50	32:06	48:10	51:40	1:07:44	1:36:19	2:15:28	2:40:32	4:18:20	5:21:03	8:36:40
5:20	16:34	26:31	26:40	33:08	49:43	53:20	1:09:55	1:39:25	2:19:50	2:45:42	4:26:40	5:31:25	8:53:20
5:30	17:05	27:20	27:30	34:11	51:16	55:00	1:12:06	1:42:32	2:24:12	2:50:53	4:35:00	5:41:46	9:10:00
5:40	17:36	28:10	28:20	35:13	52:49	56:40	1:14:17	1:45:38	2:28:34	2:56:04	4:43:20	5:52:08	9:26:40
5:50	18:07	29:00	29:10	36:15	54:22	58:20	1:16:28	1:48:45	2:32:57	3:01:15	4:51:40	6:02:29	9:43:20
6:00	18:39	29:50	30:00	37:17	55:56	1:00:00	1:18:39	1:51:51	2:37:19	3:06:25	5:00:00	6:12:50	10:00:00
6:10	19:10	30:39	30:50	38:19	57:29	1:01:40	1:20:50	1:54:58	2:41:41	3:11:36	5:08:20	6:23:12	10:16:40
6:20	19:41	31:29	31:40	39:21	59:02	1:03:20	1:23:02	1:58:04	2:46:03	3:16:47	5:16:40	6:33:33	10:33:20
6:30	20:12	32:19	32:30	40:23	1:00:35	1:05:00	1:25:13	2:01:10	2:50:25	3:21:57	5:25:00	6:43:55	10:50:00
6:40	20:43	33:08	33:20	41:26	1:02:08	1:06:40	1:27:24	2:04:17	2:54:48	3:27:08	5:33:20	6:54:16	11:06:40
6:50	21:14	33:58	34:10	42:28	1:03:42	1:08:20	1:29:35	2:07:23	2:59:10	3:32:19	5:41:40	7:04:37	11:23:20
7:00	21:45	34:48	35:00	43:30	1:05:15	1:10:00	1:31:46	2:10:30	3:03:32	3:37:29	5:50:00	7:14:59	11:40:00
7:10	22:16	35:38	35:50	44:32	1:06:48	1:11:40	1:33:57	2:13:36	3:07:54	3:42:40	5:58:20	7:25:20	11:56:40
7:20	22:47	36:27	36:40	45:34	1:08:21	1:13:20	1:36:08	2:16:42	3:12:16	3:47:51	6:06:40	7:35:42	12:13:20
7:30	23:18	37:17	37:30	46:36	1:09:54	1:15:00	1:38:19	2:19:49	3:16:38	3:53:02	6:15:00	7:46:03	12:30:00
7:40	23:49	38:07	38:20	47:38	1:11:28	1:16:40	1:40:30	2:22:55	3:21:01	3:58:12	6:23:20	7:56:24	12:46:40
7:50	24:20	38:56	39:10	48:41	1:13:01	1:18:20	1:42:41	2:26:02	3:25:23	4:03:23	6:31:40	8:06:46	13:03:20
8:00	24:51	39:46	40:00	49:43	1:14:34	1:20:00	1:44:53	2:29:08	3:29:45	4:08:34	6:40:00	8:17:07	13:20:00
8:10	25:22	40:36	40:50	50:45	1:16:07	1:21:40	1:47:04	2:32:15	3:34:07	4:13:44	6:48:20	8:27:29	13:36:40
8:20	25:54	41:26	41:40	51:47	1:17:41	1:23:20	1:49:15	2:35:21	3:38:29	4:18:55	6:56:40	8:37:50	13:53:20
8:30	26:25	42:15	42:30	52:49	1:19:14	1:25:00	1:51:26	2:38:27	3:42:51	4:24:06	7:05:00	8:48:11	14:10:00
8:40	26:56	43:05	43:20	53:51	1:20:47	1:26:40	1:53:37	2:41:34	3:47:14	4:29:16	7:13:20	8:58:33	14:26:40
8:50	27:27	43:55	44:10	54:53	1:22:20	1:28:20	1:55:48	2:44:40	3:51:36	4:34:27	7:21:40	9:08:54	14:43:20
9:00	27:58	44:44	45:00	55:56	1:23:53	1:30:00	1:57:59	2:47:47	3:55:58	4:39:38	7:30:00	9:19:16	15:00:00
9:10	28:29	45:34	45:50	56:58	1:25:27	1:31:40	2:00:10	2:50:53	4:00:20	4:44:49	7:38:20	9:29:37	15:16:40
9:20	29:00	46:24	46:40	58:00	1:27:00	1:33:20	2:02:21	2:54:00	4:04:43	4:49:59	7:46:40	9:39:58	15:33:20
9:30	29:31	47:14	47:30	59:02	1:28:33	1:35:00	2:04:32	2:57:06	4:09:05	4:55:10	7:55:00	9:50:20	15:50:00
9:40	30:02	48:03	48:20	1:00:04	1:30:06	1:36:40	2:06:43	3:00:12	4:13:27	5:00:21	8:03:20	10:00:41	16:06:40
9:50	30:33	48:53	49:10	1:01:06	1:31:39	1:38:20	2:08:55	3:03:19	4:17:49	5:05:31	8:11:40	10:11:03	16:23:20

1 MILE = 1.609 KILOMETERS

PACE

Mile Pace	5K	8K	5M	10K	15K	10M	13.1M	30K	26.2M	50K	50M	100K	100M
10:00	31:04	49:43	50:00	1:02:08	1:33:13	1:40:00	2:11:06	3:06:25	4:22:11	5:10:42	8:20:00	10:21:24	16:40:00
10:10	31:35	50:32	50:50	1:03:11	1:34:46	1:41:40	2:13:17	3:09:32	4:26:33	5:15:53	8:28:20	10:31:45	16:56:40
10:20	32:06	51:22	51:40	1:04:13	1:36:19	1:43:20	2:15:28	3:12:38	4:30:56	5:21:03	8:36:40	10:42:07	17:13:20
10:30	32:37	52:12	52:30	1:05:15	1:37:52	1:45:00	2:17:39	3:15:44	4:35:18	5:26:14	8:45:00	10:52:28	17:30:00
10:40	33:08	53:02	53:20	1:06:17	1:39:25	1:46:40	2:19:50	3:18:51	4:39:40	5:31:25	8:53:20	11:02:50	17:46:40
10:50	33:40	53:51	54:10	1:07:19	1:40:59	1:48:20	2:22:01	3:21:57	4:44:02	5:36:36	9:01:40	11:13:11	18:03:20
11:00	34:11	54:41	55:00	1:08:21	1:42:32	1:50:00	2:24:12	3:25:04	4:48:24	5:41:46	9:10:00	11:23:32	18:20:00
11:10	34:42	55:31	55:50	1:09:23	1:44:05	1:51:40	2:26:23	3:28:10	4:52:47	5:46:57	9:18:20	11:33:54	18:36:40
11:20	35:13	56:20	56:40	1:10:26	1:45:38	1:53:20	2:28:34	3:31:17	4:57:09	5:52:08	9:26:40	11:44:15	18:53:20
11:30	35:44	57:10	57:30	1:11:28	1:47:11	1:55:00	2:30:45	3:34:23	5:01:31	5:57:18	9:35:00	11:54:37	19:10:00
11:40	36:15	58:00	58:20	1:12:30	1:48:45	1:56:40	2:32:57	3:37:29	5:05:53	6:02:29	9:43:20	12:04:58	19:26:40
11:50	36:46	58:50	59:10	1:13:32	1:50:18	1:58:20	2:35:08	3:40:36	5:10:15	6:07:40	9:51:40	12:15:19	19:43:20
12:00	37:17	59:39	1:00:00	1:14:34	1:51:51	2:00:00	2:37:19	3:43:42	5:14:38	6:12:50	10:00:00	12:25:41	20:00:00
12:10	37:48	1:00:29	1:00:50	1:15:36	1:53:24	2:01:40	2:39:30	3:46:49	5:19:00	6:18:01	10:08:20	12:36:02	20:16:40
12:20	38:19	1:01:19	1:01:40	1:16:38	1:54:58	2:03:20	2:41:41	3:49:55	5:23:22	6:23:12	10:16:40	12:46:24	20:33:20
12:30	38:50	1:02:08	1:02:30	1:17:41	1:56:31	2:05:00	2:43:52	3:53:02	5:27:44	6:28:23	10:25:00	12:56:45	20:50:00
12:40	39:21	1:02:58	1:03:20	1:18:43	1:58:04	2:06:40	2:46:03	3:56:08	5:32:06	6:33:33	10:33:20	13:07:06	21:06:40
12:50	39:52	1:03:48	1:04:10	1:19:45	1:59:37	2:08:20	2:48:14	3:59:14	5:36:28	6:38:44	10:41:40	13:17:28	21:23:20
13:00	40:23	1:04:38	1:05:00	1:20:47	2:01:10	2:10:00	2:50:25	4:02:21	5:40:51	6:43:55	10:50:00	13:27:49	21:40:00
13:10	40:55	1:05:27	1:05:50	1:21:49	2:02:44	2:11:40	2:52:36	4:05:27	5:45:13	6:49:05	10:58:20	13:38:11	21:56:40
13:20	41:26	1:06:17	1:06:40	1:22:51	2:04:17	2:13:20	2:54:48	4:08:34	5:49:35	6:54:16	11:06:40	13:48:32	22:13:20
13:30	41:57	1:07:07	1:07:30	1:23:53	2:05:50	2:15:00	2:56:59	4:11:40	5:53:57	6:59:27	11:15:00	13:58:53	22:30:00
13:40	42:28	1:07:56	1:08:20	1:24:55	2:07:23	2:16:40	2:59:10	4:14:46	5:58:19	7:04:37	11:23:20	14:09:15	22:46:40
13:50	42:59	1:08:46	1:09:10	1:25:58	2:08:56	2:18:20	3:01:21	4:17:53	6:02:42	7:09:48	11:31:40	14:19:36	23:03:20
14:00	43:30	1:09:36	1:10:00	1:27:00	2:10:30	2:20:00	3:03:32	4:20:59	6:07:04	7:14:59	11:40:00	14:29:58	23:20:00
14:10	44:01	1:10:26	1:10:50	1:28:02	2:12:03	2:21:40	3:05:43	4:24:06	6:11:26	7:20:10	11:48:20	14:40:19	23:36:40
14:20	44:32	1:11:15	1:11:40	1:29:04	2:13:36	2:23:20	3:07:54	4:27:12	6:15:48	7:25:20	11:56:40	14:50:40	23:53:20
14:30	45:03	1:12:05	1:12:30	1:30:06	2:15:09	2:25:00	3:10:05	4:30:19	6:20:10	7:30:31	12:05:00	15:01:02	24:10:00
14:40	45:34	1:12:55	1:13:20	1:31:08	2:16:42	2:26:40	3:12:16	4:33:25	6:24:33	7:35:42	12:13:20	15:11:23	24:26:40
14:50	46:05	1:13:44	1:14:10	1:32:10	2:18:16	2:28:20	3:14:27	4:36:31	6:28:55	7:40:52	12:21:40	15:21:45	24:43:20
15:00	46:36	1:14:34	1:15:00	1:33:13	2:19:49	2:30:00	3:16:38	4:39:38	6:33:17	7:46:03	12:30:00	15:32:06	25:00:00

1 KILOMETER = .6214 MILES

Time Factors (men)

AGE	5K	8K/5M	10K	10M	13.1M	26.2M
20-34	1.000	1.000	1.000	1.000	1.000	1.000
35	0.9963	1.000	1.000	1.000	1.000	1.000
36	0.9895	0.9934	0.9953	0.9996	1.000	1.000
37	0.9827	0.9866	0.9884	0.9928	0.9957	1.000
38	0.9760	0.9797	0.9816	0.9859	0.9888	0.9973
39	0.9692	0.9729	0.9747	0.9791	0.9820	0.9904
40	0.9624	0.9661	0.9679	0.9722	0.9751	0.9835
41	0.9555	0.9592	0.9610	0.9653	0.9682	0.9765
42	0.9487	0.9523	0.9541	0.9583	0.9612	0.9695
43	0.9418	0.9454	0.9471	0.9514	0.9543	0.9626
44	0.9350	0.9385	0.9402	0.9444	0.9473	0.9556
45	0.9281	0.9316	0.9333	0.9375	0.9404	0.9486
46	0.9211	0.9246	0.9262	0.9304	0.9333	0.9415
47	0.9141	0.9175	0.9192	0.9233	0.9262	0.9344
48	0.9071	0.9105	0.9121	0.9163	0.9192	0.9272
49	0.9001	0.9034	0.9051	0.9092	0.9121	0.9201
50	0.8931	0.8964	0.8980	0.9021	0.9050	0.9130
51	0.8859	0.8891	0.8907	0.8948	0.8977	0.9057
52	0.8787	0.8819	0.8834	0.8875	0.8904	0.8983
53	0.8714	0.8746	0.8762	0.8802	0.8831	0.8910
54	0.8642	0.8674	0.8689	0.8729	0.8758	0.8836
55	0.8570	0.8601	0.8616	0.8656	0.8685	0.8763
56	0.8495	0.8525	0.8540	0.8580	0.8609	0.8686
57	0.8419	0.8449	0.8464	0.8504	0.8533	0.8610
58	0.8344	0.8374	0.8388	0.8427	0.8456	0.8533
59	0.8268	0.8298	0.8312	0.8351	0.8380	0.8457
60	0.8193	0.8222	0.8236	0.8275	0.8304	0.8380
61	0.8113	0.8142	0.8156	0.8194	0.8223	0.8299
62	0.8033	0.8062	0.8075	0.8114	0.8143	0.8218
63	0.7954	0.7981	0.7995	0.8033	0.8062	0.8137
64	0.7874	0.7901	0.7914	0.7953	0.7982	0.8056

AGE	5K	8K/5M	10K	10M	13.1M	26.2M
65	0.7794	0.7821	0.7834	0.7872	0.7901	0.7975
66	0.7708	0.7735	0.7748	0.7786	0.7815	0.7888
67	0.7623	0.7649	0.7662	0.7699	0.7728	0.7801
68	0.7537	0.7563	0.7575	0.7613	0.7642	0.7715
69	0.7452	0.7477	0.7489	0.7526	0.7555	0.7628
70	0.7366	0.7391	0.7403	0.7440	0.7469	0.7541
71	0.7273	0.7298	0.7309	0.7346	0.7375	0.7447
72	0.7180	0.7204	0.7216	0.7252	0.7281	0.7353
73	0.7087	0.7111	0.7122	0.7159	0.7188	0.7258
74	0.6994	0.7017	0.7029	0.7065	0.7094	0.7164
75	0.6901	0.6924	0.6935	0.6971	0.7000	0.7070
76	0.6798	0.6821	0.6832	0.6868	0.6897	0.6966
77	0.6696	0.6718	0.6729	0.6764	0.6793	0.6862
78	0.6593	0.6615	0.6625	0.6661	0.6690	0.6759
79	0.6491	0.6512	0.6522	0.6557	0.6586	0.6655
80	0.6388	0.6409	0.6419	0.6454	0.6483	0.6551
85	0.5807	0.5826	0.5835	0.5869	0.5898	0.5964
90	0.5111	0.5128	0.5136	0.5169	0.5198	0.5262
95	0.4172	0.4187	0.4194	0.4226	0.4255	0.4317
100	0.2619	0.2632	0.2638	0.2669	0.2698	0.2758

How to Use the Age-Adjusted Charts: As we age past our prime running years, our times get a bit slower and our bodies a bit sorer. This table helps us deal with the former at least. It converts your current times at the most popular distances into the theoretical equivalent of what you would have done in your prime.

1. Convert your time into seconds by multiplying the minutes by 60 and adding the seconds. For example, a 60-year-old man just ran a 3:30:24 marathon so:
   (210 minutes x 60 sec.) + (24 sec.) = 12,624 seconds
2. Multiply your time in seconds by your age-adjusted factor in the table:
   12,624 seconds x 0.8380 = 10,579 seconds
3. Convert this time into hours:minutes:seconds format.
   10,579 seconds divided by 60 seconds = 176.32 minutes (which = 2hr 56.32 min)
   .32 minutes x 60 seconds = 19 seconds
   Therefore, 10,579 seconds = 2:56:19

So the 60-year-old man with a 3:30:24 marathon ran the equivalent of a 2:56:19 marathon by a runner in his prime.

AGE	5K	8K/5M	10K	10M	13.1M	26.2M	AGE	5K	8K/5M	10K	10M	13.1M	26.2M
20-34	1.000	1.000	1.000	1.000	1.000	1.000	65	0.7450	0.7485	0.7505	0.7550	0.7572	0.7660
35	0.9913	0.9954	0.9974	1.000	1.000	1.000	66	0.7355	0.7389	0.7409	0.7454	0.7476	0.7564
36	0.9835	0.9876	0.9896	0.9941	0.9969	1.000	67	0.7259	0.7294	0.7314	0.7359	0.7380	0.7468
37	0.9758	0.9798	0.9818	0.9863	0.9891	0.9979	68	0.7164	0.7198	0.7218	0.7263	0.7285	0.7373
38	0.9680	0.9721	0.9741	0.9786	0.9813	0.9901	69	0.7068	0.7103	0.7123	0.7168	0.7189	0.7277
39	0.9603	0.9643	0.9663	0.9708	0.9735	0.9823	70	0.6973	0.7007	0.7027	0.7072	0.7093	0.7181
40	0.9525	0.9565	0.9585	0.9630	0.9657	0.9745	71	0.6870	0.6904	0.6924	0.6969	0.6990	0.7078
41	0.9447	0.9486	0.9506	0.9551	0.9578	0.9666	72	0.6767	0.6801	0.6821	0.6866	0.6887	0.6975
42	0.9368	0.9408	0.9428	0.9473	0.9499	0.9587	73	0.6665	0.6698	0.6718	0.6763	0.6783	0.6871
43	0.9290	0.9329	0.9349	0.9394	0.9421	0.9509	74	0.6562	0.6595	0.6615	0.6660	0.6680	0.6768
44	0.9211	0.9251	0.9271	0.9316	0.9342	0.9430	75	0.6459	0.6492	0.6512	0.6557	0.6577	0.6665
45	0.9133	0.9172	0.9192	0.9237	0.9263	0.9351	76	0.6347	0.6379	0.6399	0.6444	0.6464	0.6552
46	0.9053	0.9092	0.9112	0.9157	0.9183	0.9271	77	0.6234	0.6267	0.6287	0.6332	0.6351	0.6439
47	0.8973	0.9012	0.9032	0.9077	0.9103	0.9191	78	0.6122	0.6154	0.6174	0.6219	0.6239	0.6327
48	0.8894	0.8932	0.8952	0.8997	0.9022	0.9110	79	0.6009	0.6042	0.6062	0.6107	0.6126	0.6214
49	0.8814	0.8852	0.8872	0.8917	0.8942	0.9030	80	0.5897	0.5929	0.5949	0.5994	0.6013	0.6101
50	0.8734	0.8772	0.8792	0.8837	0.8862	0.8950	85	0.5267	0.5298	0.5318	0.5363	0.5381	0.5469
51	0.8652	0.8690	0.8710	0.8755	0.8780	0.8868	90	0.4522	0.4552	0.4572	0.4617	0.4634	0.4722
52	0.8570	0.8608	0.8628	0.8673	0.8697	0.8785	95	0.3534	0.3563	0.3583	0.3628	0.3644	0.3732
53	0.8488	0.8525	0.8545	0.8590	0.8615	0.8703	100	0.1932	0.1960	0.1980	0.2025	0.2040	0.2128
54	0.8406	0.8443	0.8463	0.8508	0.8532	0.8620							
55	0.8324	0.8361	0.8381	0.8426	0.8450	0.8538							
56	0.8239	0.8276	0.8296	0.8341	0.8364	0.8452							
57	0.8154	0.8190	0.8210	0.8255	0.8279	0.8367							
58	0.8068	0.8105	0.8125	0.8170	0.8193	0.8281							
59	0.7983	0.8019	0.8039	0.8084	0.8108	0.8196							
60	0.7898	0.7934	0.7954	0.7999	0.8022	0.8110							
61	0.7808	0.7844	0.7864	0.7909	0.7932	0.8020							
62	0.7719	0.7754	0.7774	0.7819	0.7842	0.7930							
63	0.7629	0.7665	0.7685	0.7730	0.7752	0.7840							
64	0.7540	0.7575	0.7595	0.7640	0.7662	0.7750							

TREADMILL

MPH Setting on Treadmill	Flat Road Pace*	Equivalent Pace-Per-Mile on Various Incline Settings on the Treadmill										
		0%*	1%	2%	3%	4%	5%	6%	7%	8%	9%	10%
5.0	12:00	12:31	11:44	11:05	10:32	10:03	9:38	9:16	8:56	8:38	8:22	8:07
5.2	11:32	12:02	11:18	10:42	10:11	9:44	9:20	8:59	8:40	8:23	8:08	7:54
5.4	11:07	11:35	10:55	10:20	9:51	9:26	9:03	8:43	8:25	8:09	7:55	7:41
5.6	10:43	11:10	10:32	10:00	9:33	9:09	8:48	8:29	8:12	7:56	7:42	7:29
5.8	10:21	10:47	10:12	9:42	9:16	8:53	8:33	8:15	7:58	7:44	7:30	7:18
6.0	10:00	10:26	9:52	9:24	9:00	8:38	8:19	8:02	7:46	7:32	7:19	7:07
6.1	9:50	10:15	9:43	9:16	8:52	8:31	8:12	7:55	7:40	7:26	7:14	7:02
6.2	9:41	10:05	9:34	9:08	8:44	8:24	8:06	7:49	7:34	7:21	7:08	6:57
6.3	9:31	9:56	9:26	9:00	8:37	8:17	7:59	7:43	7:29	7:15	7:03	6:52
6.4	9:23	9:46	9:17	8:52	8:30	8:10	7:53	7:37	7:23	7:10	6:58	6:47
6.5	9:14	9:37	9:09	8:45	8:23	8:04	7:47	7:32	7:18	7:05	6:53	6:43
6.6	9:05	9:29	9:01	8:37	8:16	7:58	7:41	7:26	7:13	7:00	6:49	6:38
6.7	8:57	9:20	8:53	8:30	8:10	7:52	7:35	7:21	7:07	6:55	6:44	6:34
6.8	8:49	9:12	8:46	8:23	8:03	7:46	7:30	7:15	7:02	6:50	6:40	6:29
6.9	8:42	9:04	8:39	8:17	7:57	7:40	7:24	7:10	6:58	6:46	6:35	6:25
7.0	8:34	8:56	8:32	8:10	7:51	7:34	7:19	7:05	6:53	6:41	6:31	6:21
7.1	8:27	8:49	8:25	8:04	7:45	7:29	7:14	7:00	6:48	6:37	6:27	6:17
7.2	8:20	8:41	8:18	7:58	7:40	7:23	7:09	6:56	6:44	6:33	6:22	6:13
7.3	8:13	8:34	8:12	7:52	7:34	7:18	7:04	6:51	6:39	6:28	6:18	6:09
7.4	8.06	8:27	8:05	7:46	7:28	7:13	6:59	6:46	6:35	6:24	6:14	6:05
7.5	8:00	8:20	7:59	7:40	7:23	7:08	6:54	6:42	6:31	6:20	6:11	6:02
7.6	7:54	8:14	7:53	7:34	7:18	7:03	6:50	6:38	6:26	6:16	6:07	5:58
7.7	7:48	8:07	7:47	7:29	7:13	6:58	6:45	6:33	6:22	6:12	6:03	5:55
7.8	7:42	8:01	7:41	7:24	7:08	6:54	6:41	6:29	6:18	6:09	5:59	5:51
7.9	7:36	7:55	7:36	7:18	7:03	6:49	6:37	6:25	6:15	6:05	5:56	5:48
8.0	7:30	7:49	7:30	7:13	6:58	6:45	6:32	6:21	6:11	6:01	5:52	5:44
8.1	7:24	7:43	7:25	7:08	6:54	6:40	6:28	6:17	6:07	5:58	5:49	5:41
8.2	7:19	7:38	7:20	7:04	6:49	6:36	6:24	6:13	6:03	5:54	5:46	5:38
8.3	7:14	7:32	7:15	6:59	6:45	6:32	6:20	6:10	6:00	5:51	5:42	5:35
8.4	7:09	7:27	7:10	6:54	6:40	6:28	6:16	6:06	5:56	5:47	5:39	5:32
8.5	7:04	7:22	7:05	6:50	6:36	6:24	6:13	6:02	5:53	5:44	5:36	5:29

TREADMILL

MPH Setting on Treadmill	Flat Road Pace*	0%*	1%	2%	3%	4%	5%	6%	7%	8%	9%	10%
				Equivalent Pace-Per-Mile on Various Incline Settings on the Treadmill								
8.6	6:59	7:16	7:00	6:45	6:32	6:20	6:09	5:59	5:49	5:41	5:33	5:26
8.7	6:54	7:11	6:55	6:41	6:28	6:16	6:05	5:55	5:46	5:38	5:30	5:23
8.8	6:49	7:07	6:51	6:37	6:24	6:12	6:02	5:52	5:43	5:35	5:27	5:20
8.9	6:44	7:02	6:46	6:32	6:20	6:09	5:58	5:49	5:40	5:32	5:24	5:17
9.0	6:40	6:57	6:42	6:28	6:16	6:05	5:55	5:45	5:37	5:29	5:21	5:14
9.1	6:36	6:52	6:38	6:24	6:12	6:01	5:51	5:42	5:34	5:26	5:18	5:11
9.2	6:31	6:48	6:34	6:20	6:09	5:58	5:48	5:39	5:31	5:23	5:16	5:09
9.3	6:27	6:44	6:29	6:17	6:05	5:55	5:45	5:36	5:28	5:20	5:13	5:06
9.4	6:23	6:39	6:25	6:13	6:02	5:51	5:42	5:33	5:25	5:17	5:10	5:04
9.5	6:19	6:35	6:22	6:09	5:58	5:48	5:39	5:30	5:22	5:14	5:08	5:01
9.6	6:15	6:31	6:18	6:06	5:55	5:45	5:35	5:27	5:19	5:12	5:05	4:59
9.7	6:11	6:27	6:14	6:02	5:51	5:42	5:32	5:24	5:16	5:09	5:02	4:56
9.8	6:07	6:23	6:10	5:59	5:48	5:38	5:30	5:21	5:14	5:07	5:00	4:54
9.9	6:04	6:19	6:07	5:55	5:45	5:35	5:27	5:19	5:11	5:04	4:58	4:51
10.0	6:00	6:15	6:03	5:52	5:42	5:32	5:24	5:16	5:08	5:02	4:55	4:49
10.1	5:56	6:12	6:00	5:49	5:39	5:29	5:21	5:13	5:06	4:59	4:53	4:47
10.2	5:53	6:08	5:56	5:45	5:36	5:27	5:18	5:11	5:03	4:57	4:50	4:45
10.3	5:50	6:04	5:53	5:42	5:33	5:24	5:16	5:08	5:01	4:54	4:48	4:42
10.4	5:46	6:01	5:50	5:39	5:30	5:21	5:13	5:05	4:58	4:52	4:46	4:40
10.5	5:43	5:57	5:46	5:36	5:27	5:18	5:10	5:03	4:56	4:50	4:44	4:38
10.6	5:40	5:54	5:43	5:33	5:24	5:15	5:08	5:00	4:54	4:47	4:41	4:36
10.7	5:36	5:51	5:40	5:30	5:21	5:13	5:05	4:58	4:51	4:45	4:39	4:34
10.8	5:33	5:48	5:37	5:27	5:18	5:10	5:03	4:56	4:49	4:43	4:37	4:32
10.9	5:30	5:44	5:34	5:24	5:16	5:08	5:00	4:53	4:47	4:41	4:35	4:30
11.0	5:27	5:41	5:31	5:22	5:13	5:05	4:58	4:51	4:45	4:39	4:33	4:28
11.2	5:21	5:35	5:25	5:16	5:08	5:00	4:53	4:46	4:40	4:34	4:29	4:24
11.4	5:16	5:29	5:20	5:11	5:03	4:55	4:49	4:42	4:36	4:30	4:25	4:20
11.6	5:10	5:24	5:14	5:06	4:58	4:51	4:44	4:38	4:32	4:27	4:21	4:17
11.8	5:05	5:18	5:09	5:01	4:53	4:46	4:40	4:34	4:28	4:23	4:18	4:13
12.0	5:00	5:13	5:04	4:56	4:49	4:42	4:36	4:30	4:24	4:19	4:14	4:10

* Running speed on a treadmill with no incline is actually slower than running on a flat road or track surface since you do not have to overcome air resistance on a treadmill.

NOTES

About the Author

Rich Hanna is a veteran of more than 50 marathons and ultra marathons, with a personal marathon best of 2:17. He is a two-time U.S. National 100k champion and captured the silver medal in the 2001 World 100K Championship in Cleder, France. Mr. Hanna contributes his extensive running experience as a personal running trainer and coach of the Sacramento Chapter of the Leukemia and Lymphoma Society's Team in Training marathon program. In addition, he owns and operates Capital Road Race Management, an event management and timing company based in Sacramento, California.